The American Novel series provides students of American literature with introductory critical guides to the great works of American literature. Each volume begins with a substantial introduction by a distinguished authority on the text, giving details of the work's composition, publication history, and contemporary reception, as well as a survey of the major critical trends and readings from first publication to the present. This overview is followed by a group of new essays, each specially commissioned from a leading scholar in the field, which together constitute a forum of interpretative methods and prominent contemporary ideas on the text. There are also helpful guides to further reading. Specifically designed for undergraduates, the series will be a powerful resource for anyone engaged in the critical analysis of major American novels and other important texts.

New Essays on Walden reviews Thoreau's classic from four important contemporary perspectives. Lawrence Buell explains how decisions at Houghton Mifflin (Thoreau's publisher) around the turn of the century combined with promotion of Thoreau by early Thoreauvians, literary critics, and reviewers to turn *Walden* into a classic. Nature writer and ecologist Anne LaBastille writes of her own responses to *Walden*. H. Daniel Peck examines how the pastoralism of *Walden* serves to contain not only the forces of industrialism and commerce in American society but also psychic forces in Thoreau's inner life. Finally Michael Fischer reevaluates *Walden* in the light of modern literary theory, finding that Thoreau's forthrightness in presenting and analyzing his own politics disarms his skeptical critics. In introducing these new essays, Robert F. Sayre provides a masterful short biography of Thoreau, an account of the writing of *Walden*, and a summary of other critical views. The volume will prove useful and appealing to students and professors reading *Walden* for the first time or for the hundredth time.

NEW ESSAYS ON WALDEN

★ The American Novel ★

GENERAL EDITOR

Emory Elliott
University of California, Riverside

Other books in the series:

New Essays on The Scarlet Letter
New Essays on The Great Gatsby
New Essays on Adventures of Huckleberry Finn
New Essays on Moby-Dick
New Essays on Uncle Tom's Cabin
New Essays on The Red Badge of Courage
New Essays on The Sun Also Rises
New Essays on A Farewell to Arms
New Essays on The American
New Essays on The Portrait of a Lady
New Essays on Light in August
New Essays on The Awakening
New Essays on Invisible Man
New Essays on Native Son
New Essays on Their Eyes Were Watching God
New Essays on The Grapes of Wrath
New Essays on Winesburg, Ohio
New Essays on Sister Carrie
New Essays on The Rise of Silas Lapham
New Essays on The Catcher in the Rye
New Essays on White Noise
New Essays on The Crying of Lot 49
New Essays on The Last of the Mohicans

New Essays on Walden

Edited by
Robert F. Sayre

Published by the Press Syndicate of the University of Cambridge
The Pitt Building, Trumpington Street, Cambridge CB2 1RP
40 West 20th Street, New York, NY 10011-4211, USA
10 Stamford Road, Oakleigh, Victoria 3166, Australia

First published 1992

Printed in the United States of America

Library of Congress Cataloging-in-Publication Data

New essays on Walden / edited by Robert F. Sayre.
p. cm. – (The American novel)
Includes bibliographical references.
ISBN 0-521-41435-0 (hardback). – ISBN 0-521-42482-8 (pbk.)
1. Thoreau, Henry David, 1817–1862. Walden. I. Sayre, Robert F.
II. Series.
PS3048.N49 1992
818′.303 – dc20 92-11525

A catalog record for this book is available from the British Library.

ISBN 0–521–41435–0 hardback
ISBN 0–521–42482–8 paperback

Contents

Series Editor's Preface

In literary criticism the last twenty-five years have been particularly fruitful. Since the rise of the New Criticism in the 1950s, which focused attention of critics and readers upon the text itself – apart from history, biography, and society – there has emerged a wide variety of critical methods which have brought to literary works a rich diversity of perspectives: social, historical, political, psychological, economic, ideological, and philosophical. While attention to the text itself, as taught by the New Critics, remains at the core of contemporary interpretation, the widely shared assumption that works of art generate many different kinds of interpretations has opened up possibilities for new readings and new meanings.

Before this critical revolution, many works of American literature had come to be taken for granted by earlier generations of readers as having an established set of recognized interpretations. There was a sense among many students that the canon was established and that the larger thematic and interpretative issues had been decided. The task of the new reader was to examine the ways in which elements such as structure, style, and imagery contributed to each novel's acknowledged purpose. But recent criticism has brought these old assumptions into question and has thereby generated a wide variety of original, and often quite surprising, interpretations of the classics, as well as of rediscovered works such as Kate Chopin's *The Awakening,* which has only recently entered the canon of works that scholars and critics study and that teachers assign their students.

The aim of The American Novel Series is to provide students of American literature and culture with introductory critical guides to

American novels and other important texts now widely read and studied. Each volume is devoted to a single work and begins with an introduction by the volume editor, a distinguished authority on the text. The introduction presents details of the work's composition, publication history, and contemporary reception, as well as a survey of the major critical trends and readings from first publication to the present. This overview is followed by four or five original essays, specifically commissioned from senior scholars of established reputation and from outstanding younger critics. Each essay presents a distinct point of view, and together they constitute a forum of interpretative methods and of the best contemporary ideas on each text.

It is our hope that these volumes will convey the vitality of current critical work in American literature, generate new insights and excitement for students of American literature, and inspire new respect for and new perspectives on these major literary texts.

Emory Elliott
University of California, Riverside

1

Introduction

ROBERT F. SAYRE

AS WE approach the 150th anniversary of Thoreau's stay at Walden Pond, which started on July 4, 1845, two matters become increasingly clear: first, the importance of Thoreau as a profoundly original and independent American writer, and second, the continuing difficulty people have in reading *Walden* and arriving at its meanings. In other words, *Walden* is a great book, but it is also a hard one. How could it be otherwise? The issues it confronts, like "the essential facts of life," include hard facts, not just simple facts. Moreover, we now realize that autobiographical writing, which many people once considered easy and straightforward and even unworthy of really creative writers, can be extremely difficult to write and to read, and *Walden* especially so. At the same time, nature writing, which once seemed the most genteel and noncontroversial kind of literature ("Absolutely the safest thing to get your emotional reactions over is NATURE," said D. H. Lawrence in the 1920s) is now some of the most prophetic writing of our time. It, too, can be complex, raising basic questions about knowledge, perception, and representation.

This collection of essays attempts to face these two sometimes different and sometimes related matters of *Walden*'s great importance and its numerous challenges to and difficulties for its readers.

I want to thank Richard Lebeaux, H. Daniel Peck, Lawrence Buell, and Robert Gross for their advice on the makeup and preparation of this volume (though the final decisions were mine) and to thank two graduate research assistants at the University of Iowa: Konan Amani, who provided able assistance in locating books and articles, and Dallas Liddle, a great proofreader and style checker.

1

The future author of *Walden* was born July 12, 1817, in Concord, Massachusetts, the third child of John and Cynthia (Dunbar) Thoreau. His grandfather, Jean Thoreau, a descendant of French Huguenots, had come to Boston from the Isle of Jersey in 1773, just in time to serve in the Revolution on privateers. He later became a prosperous merchant. His mother's family had also been relatively wealthy: Grandfather Asa Dunbar was a minister and then a lawyer; grandmother Mary Jones Dunbar came from a well-to-do Loyalist family in Weston, Massachusetts. By 1817, however, John and Cynthia Thoreau had declined in status. John was a modest shopkeeper who liked to read and to chat with his customers. Cynthia took in boarders. But Cynthia, who was a head taller than her husband, also was a leader in philanthropic organizations and a mother who kept her four children (Helen, born 1812; John [Jr.], b. 1815; Henry; and Sophia, b. 1819) very close to her. None ever married, or lived far from home.[1]

Thus it is quite likely, as Richard Lebeaux has argued in *Young Man Thoreau,* that David Henry, as he was christened, lacked examples of strong male authority.[2] His closest companion was his older brother, the two of them going on walks together, calling each other by Indian names, and sometimes conversing in Cooperesque mock-Indian speech.[3] In 1828 they enrolled together in Concord Academy, where, Henry later said, "I was fitted, or rather made unfit, for college, . . . mainly by myself, with the countenance of Phineas Allen, Preceptor."[4] Allen, an 1825 graduate of Harvard, taught the classical authors, geography, history, and sciences, and gave special attention to composition and debate. Thoreau was serious and scholarly, and it was he, not his brother, who the family decided in 1833, should go on to Harvard. Brother John, considered to have more all-around promise, would contribute to the tuition by teaching school, as would their sister Helen; the balance of the tuition would come from a pencil-making business father John had inherited from one of the Dunbar relatives and which had begun to succeed, and from small contributions from two aunts.[5]

At college Thoreau was a serious student, going beyond the

required curriculum by studying modern languages and attending lectures on natural history and various sciences, but he was still not exceptional. One classmate later remembered him as "cold and unimpressionable." Yet at the end of his first year he was one of five students in his class elected to the Institute of 1770, a social club and debating society. In the winter of 1835–36 he took off for one term to teach school in Canton, Massachusetts, where he boarded with Orestes Brownson and studied German with him. Those weeks of intellectual companionship, he wrote later, "were an era in my life – the morning of a new Lebenstag." Following another short absence because of an illness that may have been tuberculosis, he returned to Harvard and graduated on schedule with the class of 1837, nineteenth of approximately fifty students. His part in the commencement festivities was a short speech criticizing "The Commercial Spirit of Modern Times," a prophetic topic for him to have chosen but also a rather conventional one at that time. In the year 1837 there was a financial panic, followed by a depression, and many Americans were anxious about the growth of industrial capitalism. On August 31, the day after commencement, Emerson delivered his "American Scholar" talk to the Phi Beta Kappa society, calling for a new American intellectual self-reliance. But it is likely that Thoreau had skipped the crowds and already started home.[6]

In the following years, however, Emerson became Thoreau's mentor and exemplar. Emerson's questions on October 22, 1837, "What are you doing now? Do you keep a journal?" led him to start one that day.[7] Emerson welcomed him into the "Hedge Club," the informal gathering of New England Transcendentalists who met from time to time in Emerson's study.[8] And it was Emerson who solicited his early poems and essays for *The Dial,* the Transcendentalist quarterly that first appeared in 1840.[9] Thoreau was, as many people have pointed out, Emerson's ideal American Scholar, independently learning from Nature, the Past, and Action, and adopting Emerson's conceptions of them, as well as his conceptions of language and the self.

At the same time Thoreau, now calling himself Henry David, was also becoming his own scholar. In September, 1838, he took over the little Concord Academy and proceeded to make it such a success that in 1839 his brother came to teach with him. That August the two of them set off on a two-week excursion on the Concord and Merrimack Rivers in their homemade boat, the *Musketaquid.* He and John were both outdoorsmen, and one of their innovations as scholar-teachers, in addition to refusing to use corporal punishment, was to take the children on Saturday field trips. For this he and John were long remembered fondly by their students, including the young Louisa May Alcott.[10] That same year he and John both fell in love with Ellen Sewall, the seventeen-year-old sister of one of their students.

In April, 1841, however, they closed the Academy, mainly because of John's poor health,[11] and for the next few years Thoreau was increasingly beset by questions of vocation. For a college graduate of his time not to go into one of the respectable, lucrative professions was highly unusual, and though he had ambitions of becoming a writer and lecturer like Emerson, he was far from being able to support himself that way. One choice, offered by fellow Transcendentalists, was to join the Brook Farm utopian community. But he rejected it. "I had rather keep bachelor's hall in hell than go to board in heaven," he wrote in his *Journal* (March 3, 1841). For the next two years he lived in the Emersons' house, serving as handyman and gardener, and taking advantage of his mentor's extensive library. He was dexterous around the house and as skillful with tools as Emerson was clumsy.[12] He also thought of buying a rundown farm or going to live by Flint's Pond in Lincoln – possibilities referred to briefly in *Walden.*

Adding to his distress was the death on January 11, 1842, of his brother John, from lockjaw. For weeks, in sympathy and anguish, Henry experienced the same symptoms. The funeral sermon on John, speaking of his fondness for walks and knowledge of birds and flowers, his kindness to children and animals, his "voice to speak for all classes of suffering humanity," and even his religious unorthodoxy, could have been read twenty years later for Henry, Walter Harding wrote.[13] The brothers were that similar. John had been more gregarious and widely liked, less scholarly and aloof, and (some gossips surely said) the brother who worked.

In May, 1843, Emerson came to Henry's aid again, arranging for him to tutor his brother William Emerson's children on Staten Island, New York. Thoreau stayed there for over six months and became acquainted with Horace Greeley, Henry James, Sr., William Tappan, and other prominent literary and liberal New Yorkers. In December, however, he was back in Concord for keeps, having found Judge William Emerson's household "glazed" and lifeless and New York "a thousand times meaner than I could have imagined."[14]

He was further distressed when, on April 30, 1844, he accidentally burned 300 acres of Concord woods. He and his friend Edward Hoar had lit a fire in a dry stump, in the midst of a field, to cook some fish they had caught, and the fire ignited the surrounding grass, then spread rapidly. For years afterwards some of the owners called out "burnt woods" when they saw him, and the depth of his own guilt can be inferred from the fact that he did not write about the episode in his *Journal* until 1850, six years later. In that remarkable account (May 31, 1850), he writes of how, having spread the alarm, he suddenly ceased to believe he had done wrong, deciding the "flames are but consuming their natural food" and "it was a glorious spectacle, and I was the only one there to enjoy it." His life as an unemployed or under-employed writer, in a tight-fisted small town, where nearly every person's character and actions were always in view, must sometimes have been intolerable. Merely walking down the street, as he wrote in "The Village," could be like running the gauntlet.

Just as words could hurt, however, in the form of gossip and "impertinent" questions, they could also heal, and one of the functions of Thoreau's writing was as a kind of private therapy. It provided an arena in which he could defend himself and counter the attacks of his townsmen. It was a setting in which to meditate and continue to absorb the therapeutic influences of nature. It was a perfect complement to his walks and his solitude.

Thus one of the purposes of going to Walden was to write: first to write the meditative, discursive travel book organized around his river trip with his brother and then to write a second book about the Walden experience itself.

And write he did – clear proof that he did not pass his time just hoeing beans and gazing at the pond. By the time he left in September, 1847, he had finished the first draft of *A Week on the*

Concord and Merrimack Rivers and the first version of *Walden*. By early 1848 he also had a lecture ready "on the relation of the individual to the State,"[15] which responded to his arrest in July, 1846, for nonpayment of his poll tax; and by early summer he had finished an article on "Ktaadn and the Maine Woods," based on his trip to Maine in September of 1846. The lecture later became his essay "Civil Disobedience," and the Ktaadn piece eventually became the first part of *The Maine Woods*.

A Week, published May 30, 1849, was by no means the success he needed to launch a real career for himself as a writer, traveler, and lecturer. The book received some prominent reviews – on the front page of Horace Greeley's New York *Tribune*, in *Godey's Ladys Book*, the New York *Literary World*, and in England in the *Athenaeum* and *Westminster Review* – but the reviewers generally mixed their praise of the book's freshness and beauty with reservations about the author's Transcendentalism and "Pantheistic egotism." James Russell Lowell, Thoreau's former Harvard classmate, wrote a long piece in the *Massachusetts Quarterly Review* in which he spoke of the book's "great charm" yet joked that its digressions were like "snags" in the river. A year before, in his satiric poem "A Fable for Critics," Lowell had also joked about Thoreau following Emerson "as close as a stick to a rocket, / His fingers exploring the prophet's each pocket." Unfairly, *A Week* became something of a joke too, a book not to buy and read but just to make fun of. Hawthorne wrote to Melville that he was considering writing "A Week on a Work-Bench in a Barn."[16]

Four years later, when the publisher sent him the unsold 706 copies (out of 1,000 printed), Thoreau responded with a little grim humor himself. "I have now a library of nearly nine hundred volumes," he wrote in his *Journal*, "over seven hundred of which I wrote myself" (October 27, 1853).

2

The failure of *A Week* had a direct effect on the writing of *Walden*. First, the publisher, Munroe & Co., lost all interest in publishing *Walden*, even though it had been advertised in a back page of *A*

Week, with the result that Thoreau had time in which to return to the manuscript and substantially add to it, approximately doubling its length. As Lyndon Shanley revealed in *The Making of Walden,* the book went through seven different versions (not counting a final printer's copy done in 1854), and most of the additions were made after 1851. Second, Thoreau was forced to make changes in his own literary and personal plans, and these broadened the book's vision.

Among American classics, perhaps only *Leaves of Grass* went through so many different versions, and study of the *Walden* manuscript, which has now been done by Ronald Earl Clapper, by Stephen Adams and Donald Ross, Jr., and by Robert Sattelmeyer,[17] as well as Shanley, has been very informative. The early versions, written at the pond and shortly after, were used by Thoreau as material for lectures. They explained his reasons for going to Walden and contained his attacks, or counterattacks, on the commercialism and conformity of his fellow citizens. The writing from these versions survives mostly in the first seven chapters – "Economy" and "Where I Lived and What I Lived For" through "The Bean-Field." (We speak in terms of chapter titles though the chapter divisions were not made until 1852–53.) In this incarnation the book was mainly satire and social criticism. Based in his simple cabin, the author exposed the shams and delusions of the mass of men.

Added later, primarily after 1851, was most of the material of Chapters 8 through 18, "The Village" through "Conclusion." These chapters build up and fill out the seasonal cycle, latent in the early versions but incomplete, since they were set mainly in summer and spring. "Former Inhabitants; and Winter Visitors" was added. "House-Warming" was improved to give more attention to fall and the coming of winter. "Brute Neighbors," "Winter Animals," and "The Pond in Winter" were significantly expanded. "The Ponds," Chapter 9, was vastly enlarged, so that it became a companion to "The Pond in Winter." In like manner, other chapters and passages were consciously paired. Just as these changes worked to bring out the cycle of the year, chapters like "Sounds" and "The Bean-Field" and "The Village" were revised to emphasize the cycle of the day. Collectively, these changes developed the seasonal and cyclical structures of *Walden*, the formal elements many readers have long found attractive.

The reasons for these additions were not only aesthetic. Behind them, as Robert Sattelmeyer[18] has argued, were some deep personal changes. By 1849 Thoreau and Emerson were no longer close. Emerson had returned from Europe in 1848 enthusiastic about English material progress, and Thoreau found him too worldly. He also resented his former mentor's refusal to review and help promote *A Week*. On his side, Emerson had disapproved of Thoreau's refusal to pay his taxes, calling it "run[ning] amuck against the world,"[19] and now found Thoreau narrow and lacking in ambition. Instead of becoming "an engineer for America," Thoreau was content just to be "captain of a huckleberry party."

By 1850 Thoreau had also begun a much more comprehensive and rigorous study of natural history and of American Indian cultures and their relation to nature. From Louis Agassiz, whom he had known since 1847, he acquired a greater interest in fieldwork and taxonomy.[20] He bought botanical and zoological reference works and began serious collecting and drying of specimens. His collection of Indian arrowheads also grew, and his reading about Indians, which had once been limited to accounts by seventeenth-century New Englanders, expanded into a systematic reading of the entire *Jesuit Relations*, travelers to all parts of America, and books on native people around the world. In the three years up to November 1850, he had copied down in his "Indian Books," as he called them, about 150 pages of notes and extracts on this reading. In the four years between November 1850 and December 1854 he wrote 1,087 pages.[21] In the summer of 1853 he returned to Maine, this time to travel with an Indian guide, Joe Aitteon, who at moments gave him a vivid sense of Indian life and the "purely wild and primitive American sound," as he called the Abenaki language.[22]

With these new interests came changes in his daily routine. His mornings were for writing, his afternoons for long walks, and his evenings for reading. The writing was, typically, in his *Journal*, which was beginning to grow into a long, comprehensive, independent work, mixing his nature observations with his historical, ethnographic, and botanical reading and his notes and comments on life in Concord. All this contributed to the new manuscript of *Walden,* which uses material not just from 1845–47 but down to 1854. Thus in *Walden* social criticism, autobiography, moral philosophy, and natural history are all integrated, making a book with many different facets and themes but which most readers find brilliantly unified. In addition, its range of references is encyclopedic, taking in both Oriental and Western classics, naturalists, historians, and travelers to all parts of the globe. As recent literary historians have shown, it also contains satiric references to much of the popular literature of the nineteenth century: novels, success manuals, architectural pattern books, and agricultural journals.[23] It is a rich and allusive book.

3

When *Walden* was finally published, August 9, 1854, it met a much better reception than *A Week* did. Early reviews were numerous and almost entirely favorable. Thoreau, the reviewers decided, was a "hermit," "the young Concord hermit," "the philosophic hermit," but he was also "shrewd and sensible," full of "good hard common-sense," and a welcome new influence against "the popular tendency towards artificialities."[24] As the reviewer in the widely circulated *Graham's Magazine* put it,

> Whatever may be thought or said of his curious volume, nobody can deny its claims to individuality of opinion, sentiment, and expression. Sometimes strikingly original, sometimes merely eccentric and odd, it is always racy and stimulating. . . . He differs from all mankind with wonderful composure; . . . and occasionally he obtains a startling paradox, by the simple inversion of a stagnant truism. . . . We feel, in reading him, that such a man has earned the right to speak of nature, for he has taken her in all moods, and given the same "frolic welcome" to her "thunder and her sunshine."[25]

Within a year, the first printing of two thousand copies was nearly sold out.[26]

The modest success of *Walden,* combined with Thoreau's growing fame as an antislavery speaker, brought him new friends and disciples, some of whom would be very important to his later reputation. Franklin Benjamin Sanborn, still just a Harvard student in 1854, made several pilgrimages to Concord to meet Emerson and Thoreau, opened a school in Concord in 1855, and eventually became a prominent abolitionist, editor of the *Springfield Republican,* and author of a biography of Thoreau (1882). Daniel Ricketson, a Quaker lawyer from New Bedford, Massachusetts, became a kind of spiritual brother, writing to Thoreau from the "shanty" he had built in his backyard.[27] Thomas Cholmondeley (pronounced "Chumly"), an English author and traveler, first came to Concord in 1854 to meet Emerson, but on meeting Thoreau, liked him so much that he temporarily moved into the Thoreau household. In mid-October, the two of them, accompanied by H. G. O. Blake, a Worcester, Massachusetts, schoolteacher, hiked to the top of Mount Wachusett.[28] Blake would later be the first editor of Thoreau's *Journal,* dividing it into different volumes for each season, and further publicizing Thoreau as a nature writer.

Nevertheless, it was Emerson who, on Thoreau's death in 1862 from tuberculosis, had the greatest influence on his later reputation and on interpretations of *Walden.* At the family's request, Emerson gave the funeral eulogy, which was later published, with a few changes, in the *Atlantic.* Reprinted in Emerson's works and elsewhere, it is surely the most famous essay on Thoreau. Emerson also prepared the first edition of Thoreau's letters, *Letters to Various Persons* (Boston, 1865). The result was a further linking of the two men, something that would at times enhance Thoreau's reputation. But by further filling out the image of Thoreau as a stoical, philosophical hermit, telling many anecdotes about him and his wit, and lamenting that Thoreau had not done more, leaving "in the midst his broken task which none else can finish," Emerson seemed at the same time to diminish his achievement.

The story of how Thoreau's reputation grew over the next fifty years is carefully told by Lawrence Buell in the essay that follows, "Henry Thoreau Enters the American Canon." Buell largely rejects the myths of a neglected genius gradually winning respect from later generations – the narrative line that is the thread of most reputation studies – and looks at the convergence of commercial and ideological motives that put Thoreau into Houghton Mifflin book lists and into histories of American literature. As modern canon studies aim to do, Buell's essay teaches us not only about Thoreau and *Walden*, it also tells us about late nineteenth- and early twentieth-century American literary culture, thus giving us further perspective on our own. Buell shows that readers like the influential Bliss Perry were much less interested than we are in appraising and interpreting individual texts. They were primarily interested in Thoreau as a man, a man who embodied significant American virtues and who was to be to the reader like "a voice, . . . a companion, sharing his love of nature." They were not likely to see difficulties in understanding *Walden*. To them it was an assembly of more or less discrete nature descriptions. Buell also notes, however, that beginning around the time of the First World War, an "oppositional canon" began to form that made Thoreau (and other American writers) less genteel and more politically radical.

One of the leaders of this movement was John Macy, author of *The Spirit of American Literature* (1913), who vigorously promoted "Civil Disobedience" and Thoreau's antislavery writings over his nature writing. The political essays possessed the "flaming eloquence of his social philosophy," Macy said, whereas the nature writing was safely respectable and noncontroversial.[29] F. B. Sanborn, the abolitionists, and various late nineteenth-century reformers had also liked Thoreau the political radical, and their influence was very significant. Thoreau's first British biographer, Henry S. Salt, was a socialist and vegetarian as well as a naturalist, and a member of vegetarian groups with which the young Gandhi sometimes ate in London. It is generally believed that Salt and his biography introduced Gandhi to the essay (and concept of) "Civil Disobedience."[30] Macy's implication that a reader of Thoreau must somehow choose between the nature writing and the political writing was more reductive than most of these earlier positions. Macy helped rescue Thoreau from mere gentility by focusing on his dissent, but he also helped blinker many readers to the profound political implications of *Walden*.

In the period from the First to the Second World Wars, Thoreau, the opponent of American conformity and materialism, was very popular with younger critics. In July 1917 the editors of the prestigious new *Seven Arts* magazine – James Oppenheim, Waldo Frank, Van Wyck Brooks, and Randolph Bourne – recognized Thoreau "the conscientious objector," calling him "a perpetual reminder, the most vivid reminder our history affords us, that it is the toughness, the intransigence of the spiritual unit who alone gives edge to democracy."[31] In 1926 Lewis Mumford, in *The Golden Day,* a book very influential in the formation of the later idea of the nineteenth-century American canon, presented Thoreau as the true American pioneer, who showed "what the pioneer movement might have come to if this great migration had sought culture rather than material conquest, and an intensity of life rather than the mere extension of the continent."[32]

By 1941, when F. O. Matthiessen published *The American Renaissance,* Thoreau was definitely regarded as one of the major nineteenth-century American authors. Matthiessen did not devote as much space to Thoreau as to Emerson, Hawthorne, Melville, and Whitman, probably because he did not believe that Thoreau had either a tragic sense or a dedication to political action. He took delight, however, in Thoreau's language, drawn from early American explorers and naturalists, his landscape descriptions, and *Walden*'s organic metaphors and structure. Thoreau was a brilliant, independent "native craftsman" – very high praise from Matthiessen.

In *The Shores of America: Thoreau's Inward Exploration* (1958) Sherman Paul followed up on many of these points, giving *Walden* the kind of long, close reading the New Criticism had introduced into American literary scholarship. Arguing that *Walden* is a "fable of the renewal of life," Paul first located it in the Transcendentalists' revolt against the eighteenth-century mechanistic universe and in the Emersonian need to " 'stand in an original relationship to the universe.' "[33] He then guided the reader through the book, defining what Thoreau meant by "simplicity" and "economy," and opening up the major symbols – the house, the bean field, the animals, the ponds, and the melting clay in the railroad cut. For Paul *Walden* is the seed of the organic tradition in American art and culture, what he later called "the green tradition." *The Shores of America* was not only important to later readers of *Walden;* it made *Walden* a starting point for Paul's own extensive work on Louis

Sullivan and organic architecture, Hart Crane, William Carlos Williams, Charles Olson, Gary Snyder, and many other modern writers.

Other critics of the 1950s and 1960s refined many of the points made by Matthiessen and Paul about *Walden*'s symbols, ironies, and form. In addition, R. W. B. Lewis, in *The American Adam,* used Thoreau at Walden as the very ideal of the reborn new American man. Referring not just to the Adamic myth, Lewis pointed out Thoreau's many rites and fables of the rejection of convention, artifice, age, and meaningless tradition in favor of the natural, the fresh, the individual, and the true. Thus *Walden* won favor not only with the critical formalists in American English departments, but also with "myth critics," Jungians, and Freudians.

In 1965 Walter Harding published *The Days of Henry Thoreau,* the biography which is still the standard reference for the facts of Thoreau's life. Though Harding is an enthusiastic Thoreau follower, who has devoted his life to studying and editing his work, he is not an idolator. His tireless collecting of day-to-day details, combined with his research into collateral information about Concord and Thoreau's friends and family, laid a foundation for later critical writing, as well as for more psychologically inquiring biographies like Richard Lebeaux's *Young Man Thoreau* (1977) and *Thoreau's Seasons* (1984).

Harding was also the first editor-in-chief of the new edition of *The Writings of Henry D. Thoreau,* which began in 1971 with J. Lyndon Shanley's text of *Walden* and is now gradually bringing out a new edition of the *Journal.* The meticulous work on Thoreau manuscripts which the *Writings* requires has, in turn, facilitated such work as William Howarth's *The Book of Concord,* Robert Satelmeyer's *Thoreau's Reading,* and continued biographical research.

4

It is helpful to have some idea of the foregoing kind of critical history of *Walden* because, as Lawrence Buell explains at the beginning of his essay, we may not otherwise realize the degree to which "our responses have been preconditioned." Even a student not specifically aware of what has previously been said or written about a text such as *Walden,* someone who "couldn't care less," has still picked up notions, heard tell of it, and then had it presented in the framework of a college course, the format of a textbook, and the atmosphere of a classroom.

In the case of *Walden* yet another kind of influence has been at work, the influence of Thoreau cultists, Walden Pond pilgrims, and *Walden* imitators.[34] No other nineteenth-century American author has nearly so large or various a following; Thoreau not only wrote a book but lived at and celebrated a place that could become a shrine. With "Civil Disobedience" he affected the worlds of politics, pacifism, and social protest. The Thoreau Society, its secretary Walter Harding said many years ago, "is the only literary society I know of where the professional teachers of literature are vastly outnumbered by the non-professionals."[35]

Anne LaBastille's tribute to Thoreau expresses some of the experiences of these readers. Significantly, she began in the same position as many students today: "As a college student . . . I found [*Walden*] drudgery and shirked assignments." In her thirties, she tried again but "usually fell asleep." A work to a large degree derived from *Walden,* Henry Beston's *The Outermost House,* was the easier, at that time more vivid, nature book which inspired her own popular first book, *Woodswoman.* Not until her forties did she begin to enjoy *Walden,* and even then not from reading it but from hearing it on a tape player. Students (and not only students) do indeed have trouble getting into *Walden!* I can add, from teaching *Walden* a few years ago in Denmark, that foreign students have still more trouble, for the same reasons LaBastille remembers – the long sentences, large vocabulary, classical allusions and quotations, and failure to get Thoreau's puns and ironies.

Yet these barriers have not stopped LaBastille from finally enjoying *Walden* and developing a sense of kinship with Thoreau that is remarkable to read about. Some readers may object to LaBastille's familiarity. Why does she call him by his first name? What is the nature of her understanding of his writing? Where the serious reader of *Walden* measures understanding by the subtlety of interpretation, the serious imitator of the Walden experiment measures understanding by correspondences in experience – costs, architecture, living arrangements, and so on. LaBastille's account of these similarities and differences gives interesting perspectives on Thoreau, *Walden,* history, and ecological change. In addition, when one compares LaBastille's books and *Walden* with still other books like Annie Dillard's *Pilgrim at Tinker Creek,* Aldo Leopold's *A Sand Country Almanac,* and Edward Abbey's *Desert Solitaire,* one sees even more ways of evaluating the books and the experiences they recount. Just to start the argument, should nature writing be evaluated by its political effectiveness (in saving wilderness, say), by its literary refinement, or by, in Leopold's words, its "building receptivity into the still unlovely human mind"?[36]

5

Probably the most original critical study of *Walden* to be published in the last quarter century is Stanley Cavell's *The Senses of Walden* (1972). Cavell, a professor of philosophy, felt drawn to *Walden* as a work "written in an, as it were, pre-philosophical moment of its culture, a moment as yet primitive with respect to the sophistication or professionalization of philosophy."[37] Study of *Walden* then became "an obsession with me," he wrote, because it "presented itself as a response to questions with which I was already obsessed: Why has America never expressed itself philosophically? Or has it – in the metaphysical riot of its greatest literature? Has the impulse to philosophical speculation been absorbed, or exhausted, by speculation in territory, as in such thoughts as Manifest Destiny?"[38] Beginning his book with a chapter on "Words," Cavell thereupon engages in a kind of "metaphysical riot" of his own, analyzing the multiple meanings to Thoreau of *reading* and *writing* and the relations of readers, texts, writers, and worlds. Indeed, Cavell's disruption of our complacencies on these points – not to mention received interpretations of *Walden* – is so great that some people at first took him to be an American version of a French deconstructionist, but as Michael Fischer wrote in "Speech and Writing in *The Senses of Walden,*" an essay that should be read alongside his essay here,[39] Cavell is really quite different. Cavell is a skeptic, doubting the correspondences between word and thing, speech and writing, but a skeptic with a yearning or call to romanticism and transcendence. He wishes, as did Thoreau, to refresh and redeem language, not merely to deconstruct it. Thus as *The Senses of Walden* moves along, the reader's sense (and sense of *Walden*) keeps expanding. Facts are reestablished, as in Thoreau's sounding and graphing the bottom of Walden Pond, and the reader's imagination is reawakened. "The human imagination is released by fact," Cavell says at this point.[40]

The imagination can also be oppressed by facts, and that kind of contradiction is what inspired Walter Benn Michaels to write his answer to Cavell (and most of the critics since Sherman Paul), "*Walden*'s False Bottoms." Noting that Thoreau wants Walden both "bottomless," as a symbol of the infinite, and with a "tight bottom," accurately measured, as a basis for authority, Michaels refuses to be drawn in, as it were, and sympathizes with the many readers, from James Russell Lowell to the present, who find *Walden* – and the moral–philosophical positions taken in it – perplexing and inconsistent. The book "makes us nervous," he concludes.[41]

The essays by H. Daniel Peck and Michael Fischer both respond, though in different ways, to the complexities and contradictions found in *Walden* by Cavell and Michaels.

Peck attributes *Walden*'s difficulties not to its language (like Anne LaBastille) or its inconsistencies (like Michaels) but to intense conflicts within its pastoral structure. Pastorals have always been a way of working out conflicts between nature and culture, simplicity and refinement, life and death. As Leo Marx showed in his classic study, *The Machine in the Garden* (1964), the American pastoral has also been a way of establishing a "middle landscape" between technology and nature. Peck, however, following the emphasis of his recent study *Thoreau's Morning Work*,[42] sees other "crosscurrents" in the book. By comparing *Walden* to two landscape paintings by George Inness, he shows how difficult it is to define the complex mode of Thoreau's pastoralism. That pastoralism, Peck argues, enacts a process of containment – containment not only of the forces of industrialism and commerce, but also of the psychic forces of Thoreau's own inner life.

Michael Fischer, as an admirer of Cavell, turns to *Walden* to try to solve the problem Michael Rorty has called the major one in modern critical theory: the problem of reconstructing authority in an age of deconstruction. What makes *Walden* so peculiarly immune from deconstructionist attacks, which expose all moral and philosophical universals as based on or deriving from the political and temporal particulars of a given person and culture, is that Thoreau "flaunts his situatedness, thereby anticipating critics who would hold it against his universal claims." Few other writers are so open in their attacks on their readers, their satire on social custom, their demands for regeneration and renewal, and their readiness to judge others. Thoreau works to speak both "without bounds," that is, unfettered and beyond the boundaries of conventional discourse, and "within bounds," for himself. Thus *Walden*'s contradictions, troublesome to a deconstructionist like Michaels, are a recognized strategic necessity to Fischer. Thoreau wanted his readers to think for themselves, to conduct their own experiments, to examine their own lives.

In these four essays, then, we have four very different new approaches to *Walden:* Buell's canon study, LaBastille's personal testimony as a contemporary woodswoman and ecologist, Peck's approach to it as a pastoral, and Fischer's reflections on what it has to contribute to modern critical theory. These approaches complement one another very well. Buell gives us the history of how the man and his book became institutionalized. LaBastille gives the story of her conversion to the book, a personal story in most respects, but one that might not have occurred except for the previous canonization. Peck sets it in a literary tradition older than American culture that prepared a place, as it were, for both Thoreau and a contemporary writer–pastoralist like LaBastille. Fischer looks at it in a contemporary context, where it is not only pastoral and autobiography and literary masterpiece but also, as Cavell has shown us, a work of philosophy.

Yet to think of *Walden* as philosophy may seem to some readers to make it only more difficult, and a few more comments may be in order. We also need to reexamine the assumption made by John Macy and accepted by many later critics that *Walden,* as nature writing, does not have the political significance of "Civil Disobedience" and Thoreau's antislavery essays. How can *Walden* be all these things at once – philosophy, autobiography, nature writing, and social criticism? And recognizing that it is so difficult, is it really worth the effort of reading it?

I would therefore like to close this Introduction by looking at a passage in "Economy" in which Thoreau gives his own description of a "philosopher's" calling, at the same time laying out more of his reasons for undertaking the experiment of living at the pond and writing the book.

"To be a philosopher is not merely to have subtle thoughts, nor even to found a school, but so to love wisdom as to live according to its dictates, a life of simplicity, independence, magnanimity, and trust. It is to solve some of the problems of life, not only theoretically, but practically."[43] This passage, coming early in "Economy," just after Thoreau's praise of ancient philosophers as "a class than which none has been poorer in outward riches, none so rich in inward," seems to present true philosophers (and therefore Thoreau himself) as primarily teachers of voluntary poverty and simplicity. They also practice what they preach, solving "the problems of life" (essential needs for food, clothing, and shelter) by reducing their physical desires. This is what Emerson called Thoreau's stoicism.

But "love of wisdom" was elaborated on here as living a life of magnanimity and trust as well as simplicity and independence. Magnanimity: greatness of spirit, superiority to meanness and pettiness, and the courage and nobility to make sacrifices, especially for the public good. And trust: a faith in ultimate rightness and justice. These are not merely stoical virtues.

Moreover, in the next paragraph Thoreau writes about the higher aspirations of a man who has obtained the necessities. "Why has man rooted himself thus firmly in the earth, but that he may rise in the same proportion into the heavens above?" (p. 15) The organic metaphors are both strong and clear, as is the romantic sense that nature itself is teaching man to grow and to rise above his roots. From a postromantic perspective we can also see Thoreau selecting and creating this image as an expression (or creation?) of his own desire for transcendence. He, the writer, asks the question, at the same time putting it – sowing it – in the reader's mind and thus helping and challenging the reader to rise and flower and bear fruit too. Thoreau has ceased being just moral exemplar, which was what most autobiographers in the religious and Franklinian tradition were, and become moral reformer, moral activist, we might say. He has made his book a direct instrument of his audience's (and his own) transformation. The modern ecologist might add that such personal transformations are necessary because, as Wendell Berry wrote, "Our country is not being destroyed [merely] by bad politics, it is being destroyed by a bad way of life."[44] To save the earth, we need to change our lives. That is what *Walden* and other serious modern works of nature writing insist on.

How is the nature writer–autobiographer–philosopher to transform those who do not want to be transformed, elevate those of us who may already think we are elevated? Second, what is his own authority, and how can he establish it in an age of deconstruction? These are very modern questions, as Michael Fischer has noted, but they are also democratic questions that Thoreau and his contemporaries asked. They involve the freedom of people/readers to choose for themselves and the equality of author and reader. True magnanimity means having *both* the nobility and courage to help others *and* sufficient respect for others to leave them alone and not coerce them.

For answers we need to read the next paragraph of *Walden* very carefully, for it contains great magnanimity and also deals with some of the book's most difficult questions: For whom is Thoreau writing? What right has he to advise them (or us)? Should we imitate him or not?

> I do not mean to prescribe rules to strong and valiant natures, who will mind their own affairs whether in heaven or hell, and perchance build more magnificently and spend more lavishly than the richest, without ever impoverishing themselves, not knowing how they live, – if, indeed, there are any such, as has been dreamed; nor to those who find their encouragement and inspiration in precisely the present condition of things, and cherish it with the fondness and enthusiasm of lovers, – and, to some extent, I reckon myself in this number; I do not speak to those who are well employed, in whatever circumstances, and they know whether they are well employed or not; – but mainly to the mass of men who are discontented, and idly complaining of the hardness of their lot or of the times, when they might improve them. There are some who complain most energetically and inconsolably of any, because they are, as they say, doing their duty. I also have in mind that seemingly wealthy, but most terribly impoverished class of all, who have accu-

> mulated dross, but know not how to use it, or get rid of it, and thus have forged their own golden or silver fetters. (p. 16)

To whom is Thoreau writing and what gives him the right to address them? We answer for ourselves and in so doing, we grant him the authority "to speak" to us – because we have decided for ourselves whether we need to listen!

NOTES

1. Walter Harding, *The Days of Henry Thoreau* (New York: Alfred A. Knopf, 1970), pp. 3–12.
2. Richard Lebeaux, *Young Man Thoreau* (New York: Harper & Row, 1978), pp. 29–46.
3. *The Correspondence of Henry David Thoreau,* ed. Walter Harding and Carl Bode (New York: New York University Press, 1958), pp. 16–19.
4. Harding, *Days,* p. 25.
5. Ibid., p. 32.
6. Ibid., pp. 39–51.
7. *The Journal of Henry David Thoreau,* ed. Bradford Torrey and Francis H. Allen, 14 vols. (Boston: Houghton Mifflin, 1906), vol. 1, p. 3. Later references to the *Journal* will be identified by giving the date, in parentheses.
8. Harding, *Days,* p. 63.
9. Ibid., pp. 113–14.
10. Ibid., pp. 75–110.
11. Ibid., p. 87.
12. Ibid., pp. 126–31.
13. ibid., p. 135.
14. Ibid., pp. 155, 149.
15. Ibid., p. 206.
16. Ibid., pp. 249–53.
17. Ronald A. Clapper, "The Development of *Walden:* A Genetic Text," Ph.D. dissertation, University of California, Los Angeles, 1967; Donald Ross, Jr., and Stephen Adams, "The Endings of *Walden* and Stages of Its Composition," *Bulletin of Research in the Humanities,* 84, 4(Winter, 1981), 451–69; Robert Sattelmeyer, "The Remaking of *Walden,*" in *Writing the American Classics,* ed. James Barbour and Tom Quick (Chapel Hill: University of North Carolina Press, 1990), pp. 53–78.

18. Sattelmeyer, "The Remaking of *Walden*," p. 56.
19. *The Journals and Miscellaneous Notebooks of Ralph Waldo Emerson*, vol. 9, ed. Ralph H. Orth and Alfred R. Ferguson (Cambridge: Harvard University Press, 1971), p. 446.
20. Sattelmeyer, "The Remaking of *Walden*," p. 57.
21. Robert F. Sayre, *Thoreau and the American Indians* (Princeton: Princeton University Press, 1977), p. 110.
22. Henry D. Thoreau, *The Maine Woods*, ed. Joseph J. Moldenhauer (Princeton: Princeton University Press, 1972), p. 136.
23. See Richard N. and Jean Carwile Masteller, "Rural Architecture in Andrew Jackson Downing and Henry David Thoreau: Pattern Book Parody in *Walden*," *New England Quarterly*, 57, 4(December, 1984), 483–510; Robert A. Gross, "The Great Bean Field Hoax: Thoreau and the Agricultural Reformers," *Virginia Quarterly Review*, 6, 3(Summer, 1985), 483–97; Malini Schueller, "Carnival Rhetoric and Extravagance in Thoreau's *Walden*," *American Literature*, 58, 1(March, 1986), 33–45. For *Walden*'s use of travel literature, see John Christie, *Thoreau as World Traveller* (New York: Columbia University Press, 1965).
24. See the excerpts from journalistic reviews reprinted in Joel Myerson, ed., *Critical Essays on Henry David Thoreau's Walden* (Boston: G. K. Hall, 1988), pp. 18–21, 24.
25. *Graham's Magazine*, 45(Sept., 1854), 298. Quoted in Myerson, *Critical Essays*, p. 22.
26. Harding, *Days*, p. 340.
27. Ibid., pp. 343–4.
28. Ibid., pp. 346–7.
29. Michael Meyer, *Several More Lives to Live: Thoreau's Political Reputation in America* (Westport, Conn. and London: Greenwood Press, 1977), p. 19.
30. Erik Erikson, *Gandhi's Truth: On the Origins of Militant Nonviolence* (New York: W. W. Norton, 1969), pp. 146–7; Fritz Oehlschlaeger and George Hendrick, eds., *Toward the Making of Thoreau's Modern Reputation* (Urbana, Chicago, London: University of Illinois Press, 1979), pp. 5–6.
31. "Henry David Thoreau (1817–1917)," *The Seven Arts*, II(July, 1917), 383–5; reprinted in Sherman Paul, ed., *Thoreau: A Collection of Critical Essays* (Englewood Cliffs, N.J.: Prentice-Hall, 1962), pp. 9–12.
32. Lewis Mumford, *The Golden Day: A Study in American Literature and Culture* (New York: Liveright Pub. Co., 1926), pp. 107–20; reprinted in Paul, *Thoreau*, p. 13.

33. Sherman Paul, *The Shores of America: Thoreau's Inward Exploration* (Urbana: University of Illinois Press, 1958), p. 301.
34. For a rich account of this following, see Lawrence Buell, "The Thoreauvian Pilgrimage: The Structure of an American Cult," *American Literature,* 61, 2(May, 1989), 175–99.
35. "Five Ways of Looking at *Walden,*" *Massachusetts Review* 4(Autumn, 1962), 149–62; reprinted in Myerson, *Critical Essays,* p. 85. "Among regular attenders of our annual meetings," Harding wrote, "are a stockbroker, a retired letter carrier, a clergyman, an outspoken atheist, an entomologist, an ornithologist, a music teacher, an archeologist, a poet, a publishing company executive, a printer, a druggist, a socialist organizer, a hardware store owner, a church organist, the author of a book entitled *Why Work?* . . . , a telephone company executive, a novelist, a conservationist, an exponent of subsistence farming, a woman who announces that she 'covers the culture front in Brooklyn,' a professional mountain climber, a crime expert."
36. Aldo Leopold, *A Sand County Almanac* (New York: Oxford University Press, 1966), p. 295.
37. Stanley Cavell, *The Senses of Walden: An Expanded Edition* (San Francisco: North Point Press, 1981), p. xiii.
38. Ibid., p. 33.
39. Michael Fischer, "Speech and Writing in *The Senses of Walden,*" *Soundings,* 68, 3(Fall, 1985), 388–403.
40. Cavell, *Senses,* p. 75.
41. Walter Benn Michaels, "*Walden*'s False Bottoms," *Glyph,* 1(1977), 132–49; reprinted in Myerson, *Critical Essays,* pp. 131–47.
42. H. Daniel Peck, *Thoreau's Morning Work: Memory and Perception in A Week on the Concord and Merrimack Rivers, the Journal, and Walden* (New Haven: Yale University Press, 1990), especially pp. 134–58.
43. Henry D. Thoreau, *Walden,* ed. J. Lyndon Shanley (Princeton: Princeton University Press, 1971), pp. 14–15. Further references will be given in parentheses.
44. Wendell Berry, "A Few Words in Favor of Edward Abbey," in *Resist Much, Obey Little: Some Notes on Edward Abbey,* ed. James Hepworth and Gregory McNamee (Salt Lake City: Dream Garden Press, 1985), p. 10; quoted in Don Scheese, "*Desert Solitaire:* Counter-Friction to the Machine in the Garden," *North Dakota Quarterly,* 59, 2(Spring, 1991), 221.

2

Henry Thoreau Enters the American Canon

LAWRENCE BUELL

WE APPROACH a new book, especially a "great" one, hoping to have a new experience, but whether or not we think we do, we can be sure that our responses have been preconditioned by a more complicated process than we realize. The preservation of a text like *Walden* to the point that we consider it a "classic" a century later depends on at least two institutions or establishments about which the average reader thinks little. On the one hand, *Walden* receives the stamp of greatness from being commended by generations of presumably qualified readers whose opinions carry enough weight to perpetuate themselves. On the other hand, these opinions must make their way in the literary marketplace and be sustained by a series of successful publishing ventures, which in themselves can affect readerly opinion: the influence is mutual, not one-way. Though readers and publishers do not themselves create literature, they strongly affect whether and when we think a book is "great."

To think about these matters is neither natural nor pleasant. Not natural, for who wants to interrupt a good book by thinking about how one has been brought to the point of wanting to pick it up? And not pleasant, because who wants to be reminded that the sense of personal communication with a new voice across long distances, our "original" responses to a new text, are conditioned by the options that our culture presents to us? Yet the disorientation that comes from attending to these irksome peripheral issues can feed back to enrich our understanding of the book we think we have just discovered for ourselves. I hope that will be the result of reading this review of Thoreau's emergence as a "great" author. My essay differs from most contributions to collections of criticism on this author or that work in saying little about Thoreau's writing itself but concentrating instead on how Thoreau was "packaged" by the two establishments I have mentioned. I hope my readers will not only find the result helpful in understanding *Walden,* but will also be prompted by it to reflect on how the fate of any book is apt to be shaped by changing historical circumstances.

The Issues in Overview

One such circumstance which has influenced this essay, and which will loom large for many other readers for some time to come, is that the whole map of literary history has lately come to seem much blurrier than it has been since the first histories of English literature began to be written in the 1700s. It is no longer so clear who the "major" writers are, what entitles us to call them "major," what boundaries separate "major" figures from "minor" ones, or even what distinguishes a "literary" text from a "nonliterary" one. The so-called literary canon of English masterpieces, has in the past two decades been attacked as exclusionary and has been expanded to include, for example, more work by women and by nonwhite authors.[1] The novels of Nigerian writer Chinua Achebe may be more widely read in schools and colleges today than the African "classic" *Heart of Darkness* by the early modernist Joseph Conrad, whom Achebe in a famous essay sought to dislodge from the canon as a "bloody racist,"[2] though most English professors would regard Conrad as the more major figure. In this shifting cultural climate, the question of how "great" authors come to be recognized as such takes on new urgency.

Recent controversy over the shape and legitimacy of literary canons has inspired a new kind of inquiry that recalls, without echoing, older-style "reputation studies." Until recently, such studies took the form of documentary chronicles tracing a now unshakably canonical author's rise to eminence and present state of critical understanding, as measured largely by reviews and highbrow commentary by other intellectuals. More recent work tends to assume less and to range further beyond the history of literary appreciation into the economics and politics of authorship. Studies like Lawrence H. Schwartz's *Creating Faulkner's Reputation* (1988) and John Rodden's *The Politics of Literary Reputation: The Making and Claiming of 'St. George' Orwell* (1989) approach literary reputation not as a matter of unfolding recognition of an emerging classic so much as a shifting constellation of cultural artifacts created by interest groups. From this standpoint, canonicity looks more unstable, more politicized, and more dependent on contextual forces than on textual power. This vision reflects a view of canonicity as a cultural construct to be appraised coolly or suspiciously, rather than accepted as a given.

The two eras of reputation studies I have distinguished rather too neatly might be seen as necessary complements and antidotes. The documentary evidence unearthed by the older scholarship, for example, has provided much of the data base for the newer, whereas the newer work sifts that evidence with greater subtlety.[3]

Thoreau's canonization has a special interest for Americanists. For one thing, with the possible exception of Poe, Thoreau was the first case of an American author initially deemed second-rate to be "officially" promoted to canonical status. This itself makes him symptomatic of American literary distinctiveness, for the reputations of American writers have so far been much more volatile than those of the British. Many of our early authors now considered classic were not recognized as such until the twentieth century: Poe, Whitman, Melville, Dickinson. Why was Thoreau the first of these to be accepted by the literary establishment? What does his case suggest about the others? This essay provides some answers. Indeed, Thoreau's vicissitudes allow us to glimpse the whole American literary canon in the process of formation.

Thoreau and His Publisher

Thoreau often complained about the commodification of art and the neglect of the serious artist. Such complaints, like his irritation at the failure of "my publisher, falsely so called" to sell his first book, create the impression that Thoreau was unlucky in his contacts with the publishing industry.[4] The reverse was true. During his lifetime, Thoreau enjoyed the good will of two of America's most enterprising figures in literary publishing and promoting, Horace Greeley of New York and James T. Fields of Boston, both of whom were more supportive of his work than his commercial track record warranted. After his death, the Houghton Mifflin Company, successor to the firm of Ticknor & Fields, which far-sightedly bought up all the Thoreau copyrights for a modest sum during the 1870s, played a notable if not precisely measurable role in bringing about Thoreau's canonization during the next several decades. As we shall soon see, the combination of shrewd promotion and (it seems) speculative faith in Thoreau's destiny that the firm exhibited over the quarter of a century starting in the early 1880s both necessitates and calls into question the now-popular interpretation of canon formation as the work of institutional self-interest.

The start and close of our story go like this. On the eve of the period on which we shall concentrate (1880–1915), in the company's marketing policy Thoreau occupied a distinctively second-rank status. "Our book list," reads an 1879 circular, "includes the works of the most eminent and popular of American writers," among whom nine are specifically named, including Longfellow and other leading poets of the New England group (Bryant, Lowell, Holmes, Whittier), as well as Harriet Beecher Stowe and Bret Harte, but not Thoreau.[5] Indeed there was no reason to name him; Thoreau's seven volumes were selling a total of less than a thousand copies a year. By 1903, however, the firm's head, George H. Mifflin, was declaring that "Thoreau should be our next great author after Emerson."[6] This decision inaugurated the 1906 twenty-volume edition of Thoreau's collected writings, a historic publishing event commonly taken as the point of Thoreau's canonization. The inclusion of the *Journal* in fourteen volumes made Thoreau the first American person of letters to have his diary published in full.

Some aspects of this success story have been well chronicled, notably the increasing bibliography of late nineteenth-century critical commentary on Thoreau and the heroic efforts of his disciples to promote his reputation.[7] These contributions have been valuable. Their limitation is that they create a somewhat mystified version of Thoreau's rise to recognition, a version that tends either merely to register the quantitative growth of critical interest in Thoreau, or to explain it in terms of a vanguard of Thoreauvian gadflies exerting pressure on a resistant establishment. It would be more just to say that Thoreau was not canonized until he became respectable, and that his canonization was effected more by establishment forces than by an insurgent group.

Late twentieth-century American readers, for whom Thoreau's "greatness" is an accepted fact (whatever emotions of pleasure, excitement, distrust, or boredom he inspires), may find it hard to understand Mifflin's affirmation as anything other than inevitable. Yet the investment he contemplated, and for which he spared little expense, was less economically justified than was the 1879 omission of Thoreau's name from the firm's circular. Between 1880 and 1903, the sales of Thoreau's books had indeed quadrupled, but his thousands were still annually dwarfed by Emerson's ten thousands, not to mention Longfellow's hundred thousands. As it turned out, the 1906 edition seems to have brought more renown than profit to the firm. Less than two thousand copies were printed, counting both the deluxe "manuscript" edition and the plain grey-blue-bound "Walden" edition one chiefly finds today in open library stacks. Although these seem to have sold out (by subscription) within five years or so, the edition never went into trade, nor did the firm's sales of other Thoreau works measurably benefit from the venture. In fact, Houghton Mifflin's sales of Thoreau were starting to taper off as the 1906 edition was being put on the market, since all of Thoreau's works except his *Journal* entered the public domain between 1891 and 1905 and competing editions by other publishers, especially of *Walden,* had begun to appear. (In 1910 American readers could choose between at least eight different publishers' editions of *Walden* and at least two of *A Week, Cape Cod,* and *The Maine Woods.*) So far as narrowly commercial motives and benefits are concerned, therefore, it is hard to interpret Houghton Mifflin's backing of Thoreau in any other light than as a calculated risk taken in the confidence of Thoreau's greatness. By any reasonable standard the risk was significant even when one notes that it was somewhat offset by the interconnectedness of his work (as we shall note below) with other titles on the Houghton Mifflin list.

What prompted George Mifflin's decision is not a total mystery, although his exact reasoning does remain mysterious. He was influenced strongly by then *Atlantic* editor and Harvard professor Bliss Perry. In his 1935 autobiography, Perry remembered "sometimes cajoling the House against its better judgment to risk something upon a new poet or to try once more a book by some veteran whose prose was savory and yet hitherto unsalable." In particular, Perry was "inordinately proud" of persuading the firm to publish both Thoreau's *Journals* and Emerson's.[8]

So, enthusiastic intervention on behalf of artistic greatness by the forward-looking intellectual broke down the cautious, pragmatic resistance of the boss and his senior staff? Likely so, for Mifflin's private correspondence with his partners credits Perry with the initiative. Not that Mifflin can be presumed a Thoreau convert; he may never even have read Thoreau. It is entirely possible that the main reason Mifflin became zealous to establish Thoreau's greatness was his frustration at the sag in profits elsewhere on the firm's literary list. Just two days before he announced his position, Mifflin had acknowledged to a partner: "I note what you say about the Whittier copyright. We have known for some time that the amount we were paying as an annuity was an extravagant one. The truth is that the sale of Whittier is steadily declining and has been during the past ten years, and instead of increasing our rate ten years ago from $1500 to $2500 as we did, we ought to have reduced it by $1000, and then we would have been about right." Fortunately the contract would be up for renegotiation in August.[9]

It is hard to resist imagining a causal link between the decision to downgrade John Greenleaf Whittier and the decision to upgrade Thoreau, an intention Mifflin announced in the very next letter bound in the company letter book. Surely this signifies the displacement of the old genteel order that formed what might be called America's "first canon" of great authors by the new order that formed what might be called the "second canon," whose ranks included other comparatively marginal or oppositional figures like Walt Whitman and Mark Twain as well as redefined versions of originally canonized figures like Hawthorne and Emerson. Thoreau's turn-of-the-century disciples, away from the literary power centers, claimed that this shakeout was in progress, that Thoreau's stock was challenging Emerson's, for instance. To continue with the case of Whittier, his sales had dropped by more than 50 percent since their peak in the early nineties at the time of his death, yet he continued to outperform Thoreau in raw numbers, though the annuity contract constricted the publisher's profit margin. The firm continued to advertise Whittier as one of the American literary greats. The sales of Longfellow, the most eminent of the nineteenth-century New England versifiers whose popular moral idealism had earned them the nickname of the "Fireside poets," slid much more gradually. So far as Mifflin's motives were concerned, it is by no means clear that the cases of Whittier and Thoreau were connected by any other principle than the desire to keep on top of the market. His decision reflected a confidence in Thoreau's stature that none of his predecessors was so bold as to claim, but it is unlikely that he saw an aesthetic paradigm shift in the making, much more likely that he put Thoreau in the category of "American writers worth promoting."

What about Bliss Perry? His interpretation is really more important than Mifflin's, since Mifflin's judgment was guided by Perry's expertise as "literary advisor." (This self-characterization, by the way, is a pointed reminder of the increasing specialization under way during the late nineteenth century within both publishing and academe.) A vigorous promoter of Walt Whitman's literary reputation during the same era, Perry seems to have solid credentials as a canonical revisionist. His championship of Thoreau, however, does not seem to have been motivated by a desire to bring established theories of American literature into question. Neither then nor later does Perry seem to have considered that Thoreau's canonization might significantly readjust our view of what was later christened (but was already being thought of as) the American Renaissance.

Perry's views are clearly outlined in a historical sketch of *The American Spirit in Literature* published shortly after World War I. With obvious pride, he notes that "Our literature has no more curious story than the evolution of this local crank into his rightful place of mastership" – a diagnosis that, as Perry must have known, had already become formulaic in American criticism. Yet he finds the event no more than "curious" – a phenomenon he prefers to cherish as a wonder rather than try to explain – and to envision as prompting Euro-American critics to "rank him with Ralph Waldo Emerson." The greatness of Thoreau for Perry is finally that he is Emerson's peer, not the caricature but the fulfillment of Emersonianism. Hence "to the student of American thought Thoreau's prime value lies in the courage and consistency with which he endeavored to realize the gospel of Transcendentalism in his own life." Thus Thoreau exemplifies good old American individualism, whose patriotic rather than oppositional flavor Perry stresses. He describes Thoreau's support for John Brown as the culmination of Thoreau's life: "Once, toward the close of his too brief life, Thoreau 'signed on' again to an American ideal, and no man could have signed on more nobly."[10]

Perry's treatment of Thoreau in this textbook literary history is wholly in keeping with what can be constructed of his activities two decades before. We have seen him link the Emerson and Thoreau journal projects in his autobiography. In 1903, Mifflin, presumably with Perry's encouragement, also linked them in suggesting to his partners that current public interest in the much publicized centennial of Emerson's birth (marked by the firm's publication of Emerson's *Complete Writings* in twelve volumes) "will spread itself to Thoreau, and that there would be a good market for a thoroughly good edition of Thoreau." Perry might be supposed to have induced Mifflin and his staff to think in a radically new direction. His contribution was to stress (as he later did in the case of Emerson) that the unpublished journals were an unusual literary find. Mifflin continues,

> It is almost unique for writers to leave so full Journals and so interesting Journals as Thoreau has left. . . . Mr. Perry's theory is that the publication in full of the Journals will only add to the interest of the writings, and that lovers of Thoreau and his writings would attach all the more value to the completed journals, which, as I say, contain matter of the utmost interest according to his report.[11]

Perry seems to have been advocating not so much a reinterpretation as a completion of the Thoreau canon, on the ground that more is better. In so doing, Perry took a historic step in moving the standards of American literary publishing in a more "scholarly" direction. Despite its flaws, the 1906 edition, with its textual annotations and critical introduction, and coeditor Francis Allen's

Thoreau bibliography that followed two years later, testify to this. Perry's contribution was not a breakthrough in Thoreau *criticism*, however. It is no accident that he delivered almost concurrently a long public tribute to Longfellow's enduring importance. His recommendation to publish Thoreau in full was a bold stroke and his esteem for Thoreau as Emerson's peer was still avant-garde, but the basis of his interest in Thoreau was not. Significantly, one of Perry's next steps in negotiating with E. H. Russell, who owned the *Journal* manuscripts and eventually received three thousand dollars for their use, was to inquire about the possible publication of a fifth book of season-inspired perceptions ("Late Spring and Early Summer"), quarried by Thoreau's literary executor H. G. O. Blake out of the *Journals.*[12] Houghton Mifflin had published the first four in the 1880s and the 1890s, along with still another Blake compendium of *Thoreau's Thoughts.* In imagining a continuation of the series, and in advocating full publication of the *Journals* from which they came, Perry was really continuing in the same vein of Thoreau promotion the firm had already been employing for the past two decades to ride the crest of the modest Thoreau revival. In a moment, we shall look at that history in more detail.

Defining the Essential Thoreau: *Walden*'s Place

First, however, a question that seems obvious needs answering: What did Mifflin and Perry mean when they said "Thoreau"? One easily jumps to the conclusion that they thought as we do today: For all practical purposes "Thoreau" means chiefly *Walden,* and beyond that "Civil Disobedience" with perhaps a smattering of other excerpts. The late nineteenth-century view of Thoreau, however, was less *Walden* centered and less text centered than is our average understanding. To be sure, *Walden* was always Thoreau's best-selling book and by the turn of the century textbook histories of American literature had begun to recognize it as the one Thoreau volume "that can strictly be called a classic, or at least a probable classic." Most commentators, however, stressed the overall unity and interest of Thoreau's work as a whole: "Open his works almost anywhere," affirmed one enthusiast of Thoreau's nature writing, "– there are ten volumes of them now, – and even in the philosophic passages you will find loving precision of touch." In other words, not just *Walden* but the entire Thoreau corpus could provide the kind of inspiration for which Thoreau was especially noted. "If your lot be ever cast in some remote region of our simple country," writes the same critic, "he can do you, when you will, a rare service, stimulating your eye to see, and your ear to hear, in all the little commonplaces about you."[13] From this critic's standpoint, Thoreau looms up not as a series of texts between covers but as a voice, a companion, sharing his love of nature with the reader through all his volumes. Even a reader who (like the one just quoted) recognized that *Walden* was Thoreau's major work was not likely to argue that it dwarfed the rest of his output. That is certainly true of Bliss Perry's treatment of Thoreau in his literary history. Perry praises *Walden* as one of the classics, but his chief interest is in discussing Thoreau as a figure, as the expression and embodiment of certain characteristically American attitudes.

Not just in Thoreau's case but in all others, the professors and schoolteachers of the late nineteenth century who codified what might be called the first canon of American literary eminences canonized figures and their associated thematic/stylistic traits rather than individual texts. Though at times they pronounced judgment on which works by an author were "best" or "most characteristic," they tended to counsel wide encyclopedic browsing rather than highly intensive concentration, especially in a writer like Thoreau who was conceived to be an artist of passages rather than of aesthetic wholes. As the first full-length interpretative history of American literature put it, Thoreau's "most characteristic" books "are Walden and Cape Cod, which, with the poems, slightly stand out from the rest. As a rule, however, Thoreau is a remarkably even writer; his chapters were like his days, merely parts of a serene and little-diversified life." Even more aggressively *Walden*-centered appraisals ("For minute and loving description of the woods and fields, *Walden* has had no rival") tended at least by implication to encourage the reader to look elsewhere in Thoreau, since the typical ground of praise ("minute and loving description of the woods and fields") extended to most of the rest of the Thoreau corpus as well.[14] Only when it began to be questioned whether literary naturism was in fact Thoreau's leading contribution to American letters did critics begin to focus on *Walden* to the eclipse of Thoreau's other books. But we are getting slightly ahead of our story and need to return for a while to the history of Thoreau as a publishing commodity to see how the dominant image just described was kept before the public eye.

Promoting Thoreau, 1880–1906

Not until Houghton Mifflin offered the 1906 edition to subscribers as part of its library of collected editions of major American authors' works did the firm decisively promote Thoreau as a member of the pantheon. Before that, the advertising department presented the sextet of Emerson-Hawthorne-Longfellow-Lowell-Holmes-Whittier as "the six great representatives of American literature."[15] Starting as early as the 1880s, however, Houghton Mifflin made increasingly aggressive attempts to market Thoreau's work.

One, already mentioned, was the series of four season books assembled by Blake, the first of which (*Early Spring in Massachusetts*) was published in 1881. The firm also began issuing Thoreau's work in multiple editions, starting with *Walden* in 1889. By 1897, buyers could choose from among five different editions of *Walden*, and for a while sales actually surpassed those of the seven editions of Hawthorne's *Scarlet Letter*. *Cape Cod* was also issued in a deluxe, illustrated edition in 1896.

Even more important for ensuring that Thoreau would become a household word, Houghton Mifflin began anthologizing him as early as 1881, in a collection of *American Prose* edited by the firm's own Horace Scudder. The Thoreau selections were "Sounds" and "Brute Neighbors" from *Walden* and "The Highland Light" from *Cape Cod*. These three pieces are all relatively accessible, they emphasize descriptive portraiture, and they feature a comparatively mild, whimsical, noncombative persona – synchronizing well with the version of Thoreau codified in Blake's season books. In these respects, *American Prose* looks directly forward to the way in which Thoreau soon began to be packaged for school text use. In 1888 he was chosen as the first nature author to be represented in the Riverside Literature Series, a pedagogical project designed to make available "the best and purest" writing in order to effect "the formation of a taste in the reader for the best and most enduring literature."[16] Predictably, the first books in the series, issued five years earlier, had been Longfellow's *Evangeline* and *The Courtship of Miles Standish,* the dramatic version of the latter, and Whittier's *Snowbound* and *Among the Hills.* The Thoreau volume included "Wild Apples" and "The Succession of Forest Trees," as well as Emerson's eulogy on Thoreau (later distributed as part of a free promotional package to attract interest in the Walden edition). Over the next two decades, this text was the biggest Thoreau seller next to *Walden.*

Thus Thoreau would first have become known to many American readers growing up in the late nineteenth and early twentieth centuries as the author of comparatively descriptive/scientific, nonmystical and nonpugnacious essays, and through Emerson's representation of him as "the bachelor of thought and nature." Students not assigned the Riverside Thoreau volume might encounter at least "Wild Apples" in the 1892 school text *Masterpieces of American Literature,* along with Bryant's "Thanatopsis," Holmes's "The Chambered Nautilus," Emerson's "Behavior," the inevitable *Evangeline* and *Snowbound,* and many other such items. This mode of anthologizing helped to ensure the canonization of Thoreau as literary naturist-at-large rather than as the author of *Walden* specifically, and that *Walden* would be read more for its charming cameos of nature descriptions than for its much sharper criticisms of the American political and economic orders. "Sounds" and "Brute Neighbors" do imply such a critique (the passages on the intruding railroad and the ant fight, for instance), but it is not so dominant as the lyric and observational elements. Thus Houghton Mifflin's way of highlighting Thoreau was very much in line with the normalizing terms of Bliss Perry's literary history and in the spirit of Emerson's 1862 affirmation that "no truer American existed than Thoreau."[17] This centrist vision of Thoreau tallied with the preferences of late-century American book buyers. The Thoreau volume containing his political essays (including "Resistance to Civil Government") consistently sold the least well through the turn of the century.

Houghton Mifflin promoted Thoreau's reputation further by recirculating critical tributes to him as the effective founder of modern American nature writing, at the same time puffing new titles by contemporary writers, thus hatching two birds from the same egg. One of the Houghton Mifflin promotional pieces quoted a review of Charles Dudley Warner's *In the Wilderness* ("as fresh and fragrant of the woods as anything that Thoreau ever wrote"); Frank Bolles's *The Land of Lingering Snow* was said to "reveal a power of minute observation as remarkable as Thoreau's"; John Burroughs was promoted as "the same breed as Gilbert White of Selborne, as Audubon, as Thoreau"; and John Muir was touted as "the Thoreau of the Far West." Reciprocally, potential subscribers to the Walden edition were informed that the type was "the same as in the Riverby Edition of Burroughs' works."[18] In short, name-droppable Houghton Mifflin authors were used to market the works of other name-droppable authors. The publishers built an image of an emerging canon of literary nature writing with Thoreau at its head. This was especially good policy given the firm's investment in what was then called "out-of-door" literature of different kinds. Apart from Thoreau, Houghton Mifflin were the publishers of Burroughs, Muir (after 1900), Mary Austin (until World War I), Celia Thaxter, Sarah Orne Jewett, Bret Harte, Bradford Torrey, Andy Adams (*Log of a Cowboy*), popular ornithologist Olive Thorne Miller, the nature-oriented works of Charles Dudley Warner and James Russell Lowell, and of numerous other figures less well known. In the same period the contents of the firm's magazine organ, *The Atlantic Monthly*, in which many future books appeared in serial or excerpt form, also show a strong tilt toward nature writing and the sometimes overlapping genre of the rustic or backwater life.

In its sponsorship of such work, which extended also to the publication of natural history field guides, the firm was responding to a perceived climate of opinion among the reading public, a climate it had helped to create. It thus capitalized on (and helped direct) such contemporary movements as back-to-naturism (for example, the rise of scouting and wilderness camping), conservationism and preservationism, and the emergence of the "nature essay" as an established, respectable genre. The firm's policy probably also reflected particular tastes among its editorship, which down to today has included staunch naturists like Francis Allen and Paul Brooks. As we saw in the case of the decision to go ahead with the Walden edition, the role of the individual intervener in publishing decisions cannot be ignored. A similar analysis could be made for Brooks's role in publishing Rachel Carson's *Silent Spring* (1962).[19]

Reading Thoreau at the Turn of the Century

Our emphasis on publisher promotion of Thoreau has perhaps created the impression that Houghton Mifflin was solely responsible for the late-century Thoreau revival. That would surely be a great exaggeration. Publishers exert considerable influence over what the public reads (obviously, if a book isn't in print, it's read less) and the terms under which a new book is discussed (the sources most often cited to demonstrate "public" reception have always been heavily influenced by publishers' manipulations). Yet a "publisher conspiracy" theory of Thoreau's canonization is probably less true than the obverse. It would be fairer to surmise that despite Houghton Mifflin's backing he almost didn't make it. Before 1880, no book by Thoreau achieved an average sale of more than 200 copies annually; in the 1890s, the firm sold only 310 copies of its first edition of Thoreau's collected works, the ten-volume Riverside edition; and the 1906 edition was not reprinted for decades. In short, although the support of America's most prestigious literary publisher did not hurt Thoreau's cause, it was hardly the sole reason for his canonization.

Thoreauvians traditionally prefer to credit Thoreau's late-century disciples, particularly such figures as Blake, whose editorial contributions have been noted and who also popularized Thoreau's work by public readings at the Concord School of Philosophy and elsewhere; British reformer Henry Salt, who wrote the first important biography of Thoreau; the two bird-watcher essayists who edited the complete *Journals,* Bradford Torrey and Francis Allen; and the raspish, indefatigable Michigan doctor-professor, Samuel A. Jones. Their contributions were indeed significant. One also must beware, however, of overcrediting the

Thoreau vanguard. Yes, Salt had a lot to do with raising sympathetic consciousness of Thoreau as culture critic, especially abroad. Yes, Blake's nature/philosopher-oriented presentation of Thoreau as journalizer helped to establish Thoreau as America's chief literary steward of the environment. Yet contemporaries like Emerson and Thomas Wentworth Higginson had been playing fundamentally similar tunes for a quarter of a century, and their literary connections and prestige were for a generation after Thoreau's death much greater than his. Thus, though the continued entrepreneurialism of true believers was important in pushing Thoreau to the fore, it doesn't explain why he emerged when he emerged, or why the critical establishment at last acknowledged his greatness. If we lean too hard on a disciple-promotion theory we risk falling into a kind of mystification no better than alleging that Thoreau had to emerge because he was great. It is more reasonable to assume that Thoreau's advocates could not have succeeded if history weren't already running their way – meaning that the inchoate complex of social habits and attitudes we call culture was reorienting itself toward the end of the nineteenth century in such a way as to benefit Thoreau. In order to understand Thoreau's canonization, we finally have to drag the whole of American civilization in.

When we do that, we risk mystification of another sort: overgeneralizing on the basis of abstractions like "history" or "America." As a way of containing the risk, we need to sift further through the presentations of Thoreau in three dozen or so textbook codifications of American literary history that appeared between the Civil War and World War I, with a view to highlighting the strategies of justification that, at the turn of the century, underprop the new regard for Thoreau's achievements. Here, if anywhere, in these standardized compendia designed for school and college use, one finds the middle-of-the-road consensus of the educated about who the major American authors are and why. This still does not get at the grass roots reaction – the reaction, for example, of students who might have resisted these assigned readings and the teachers who assigned them – but it does present the "official" turn-of-the-century version of Thoreau.

Our study of publisher behavior has paradoxically shown that at the heart of the Houghton Mifflin institutional juggernaut, the discretionary role of the (well-placed) individual actor was crucial. As we look at the testimonies to follow, we seem to see the reverse of this, the spectacle of what appear to be individual voices blending together to create a composite picture, a late Victorian discourse of Thoreau, as it were. I say "seem," because my presentational strategy of isolating dominant motifs reinforces this impression, flattening individual nuances and minority voices. Yet dominant motifs there certainly were, the main one being the increasing tendency of these histories, after 1895, to accord Thoreau major figure status, in the form of an individual chapter or section devoted exclusively to him, comparable to the treatment of the previously canonized authors Houghton Mifflin had long been promoting.

Five specific arguments were most characteristically advanced to justify this reevaluation of Thoreau – the fact of reevaluation being in itself singled out for special comment as a most unusual phenomenon, in the spirit of Perry's remark quoted earlier: "Our literature has no more curious story than the evolution of this local crank into his rightful place of mastership." Today we take the ups and downs of American literary fortunes for granted, but in the early 1900s the idea that an author could become rather abruptly canonized seemed a striking novelty. The five specific arguments justifying Thoreau's promotion were that (1) his originality relative to Emerson's was much greater than had been supposed; (2) he was America's best and most influential nature writer; (3) he soared above mere nature writing into higher, more spiritual, realms; (4) he was a good conscientious citizen and person, not, as charged, a misanthropic crank; and (5) he was great in the courage and the character of his dissent.

The internal contradictions in this collective profile should be obvious. More on them as we proceed.

Those who stressed Thoreau's originality reversed the appraisal of the earliest literary histories, which usually pigeonholed Thoreau as Emerson's disciple, of narrower range than the master, whose chief claim to originality was "in the minutiae of description, only appreciable by professed naturalists." That neatly stratified Thoreau as mediocre and as the practitioner of a minor genre with only a specialized appeal. This continued to be a minority position. As another history condescendingly put it, "His poems of observation were good, and, like a pointer-dog, he could fix his gaze upon an object for a long time at a stretch." In the more supportive commentary of the 1890s and after, this diagnosis is recast in the form of a real tribute to Thoreau's differences from Emerson. For example: "No one has lived so close to nature and written of it so intimately, as Thoreau." The Emerson-Thoreau influence, argued another historian, wasn't one-way but mutual: "Emerson was blind to obvious processes of nature until Thoreau opened his eyes." Thoreau was indeed "the parent of the out-of-door school of writers represented by John Burroughs" and others. "Yet not the best of his disciples," continues another commentator, "can reach his upper notes."[20]

In these passages, Thoreau's status as the father of a genre of "out-of-door" literature is being noted to his credit rather than as a sign of minor status. This assessment reflects the increase in production, sales, and critical praise of nonfictional nature writing in America in the late nineteenth century, which in turn reflected the rise of preservationist and, more broadly, antiindustrialist sentiment, not to mention the influence of what has been called the heyday of natural history writing in Britain, from Gilbert White to Charles Darwin and (in a more specifically literary vein) Richard Jeffries.[21] A combination of international literary fashion and future shock seems to have helped stimulate a following of sorts for the brand of artful meditative observation featured in middle and late Thoreau, and highlighted by the season books edited by Blake.

In this respect, the priorities of the American literary establishment at the turn of the century differed from those of all other epochs of American literary history. From the standpoint of mid-nineteenth-century American literary tastemakers, the genres of the nature essay and the nature book did not exist, although nature poetry did. From a mid-twentieth-century literary historian's standpoint, they no longer existed, not because they literally didn't, but because the ordinary business of literary analysis had become more severely confined to the three traditionally fictive modes of poetry, prose fiction, and drama. Today, resurgent environmentalism and a reexpansion of the definition of what counts as legitimate literary discourse have converged with literary practice (for example, Edward Abbey, Barry Lopez, Peter Matthiessen, Annie Dillard, Wendell Berry) to confer a critical legitimacy on environmental prose that the previous generation did not enjoy. At the turn of the century, it was more possible than in the previous or next generations to take seriously Thoreau's credentials as the founder of what later came to look like a mere enclave canon.

The positing of a Thoreau-founded tradition was historically incorrect, but it was consistent with what had come to be the agreed-upon facts. Especially among the northeastern practitioners from whom the literary nature essay spread west and south, the frequency of quotation makes it clear that Thoreau had become the key American precursor. William Bartram, Thomas Jefferson, John James Audubon, Alexander Wilson, indeed all the colonial and early national natural history writers quickly faded from critical consciousness after the mid-nineteenth century. A generation after Thoreau, John Burroughs, America's leading nature essayist at the turn of the twentieth century, wrote about Thoreau in somewhat the same way eighteenth-century and romantic poets tended to write about Milton: as the imposing precursor figure whose shadow he must disown or destroy in order to establish his own legitimacy. Lesser literary naturalists paid Thoreau increasing deference, as in the following passage from Joseph Jackson's book of essays, *Through Glade and Mead* (1894):

> Thoreau led the way, and the number of his disciples is increasing, though they follow the master with unequal steps. Where a hundred persons read one of Thoreau's books on their publication, a thousand have now learned to look forward with pleasure to a new outdoor book by Burroughs. . . . What White did for Selbourne and Jeffries for Coate was done as effectually, but entirely in his own way, by Thoreau. As Aias stood preeminent among the Argives by the measure of his head and broad shoulders, so stands Thoreau among men who have loved Nature. He stands alone, not to be compared with others, for he is incomparable.[22]

These heartfelt words are also dangerous words, however, because they threaten to diminish even as they aggrandize, by linking Thoreau to a cohort that even an insider like Jackson can't seem to feel completely proud of belonging to. An 1894 reader who felt the great tide of literary naturism rising around him or her was not likely to believe in all seriousness that the scantily educated Jeffries or the pedantic White were *really* more important prose stylists than, say, Matthew Arnold or John Ruskin. To praise Thoreau as the father of a genre was helpful in securing him a niche, but not enough to secure him great writer status unless in the same breath one established his incomparableness: his transcendence of this and indeed all genres. The previous quotes praise Thoreau's ability to hit the "upper notes," to go beyond the comparatively unenterprising graceful descriptiveness that is the stock-in-trade of the average literary naturist.

The literary historians neither agreed on nor precisely specified what it was that put Thoreau in a different category from his successors. Cited were his dexterity as a verbal artist, his mysticism, his bookishness, and his cantankerous tone. The commentators groped to limn the Thoreauvian difference without, as yet, having a refined enough critical apparatus to make the necessary distinctions. For example, the intricate metaphorical structure of *Walden* was not defined until F. O. Matthiessen's *American Renaissance* (1941) pointed out the correlation between images of seasonal change and the theme of spiritual metamorphosis.[23] By comparison, turn-of-the-century commentators praised Thoreau impressionistically for possessing "the power of making sentences and paragraphs artistically beautiful," but how he accomplished it remained opaque.

A more interesting aspect of the literary historians' defense of Thoreau as more than simply a nature essayist was their periodic recourse to two final strategies of justification: the resolute normalization of Thoreau as a good citizen and respectable figure and praise of Thoreau as a social conscience. It was clearly in the interest of both these arguments to dwell up to a point on Thoreau's closeness to nature – the former stressing the charm and coziness of his rapport and portraiture, the latter his wildness as antisocial hermit. It was also in the interest of both to turn Thoreau away from nature, again for different reasons. This we can easily see by comparing the work of two quite different Thoreauvians.

Thomas Wentworth Higginson, mentioned earlier as a younger Transcendentalist and admiring friend of both Emerson and Thoreau, sought to make Thoreau look appealingly respectable to establishment literati and mainstream readers. Predictably, he began his account (1903) by locking horns with James Russell Lowell, whose 1865 critique still stood as the most imposing disparagement, being from the pen of America's still most eminent critic.[24] "Lowell accepts throughout," says Higginson, "the popular misconception . . . that Thoreau hated civilization, and believed only in wilderness." In truth, Thoreau was never "really banished from the world," nor did "he seek or profess banishment." He earned "an honest living by gardening and land-surveying"; furthermore, "his home life – always the best test – was thoroughly affectionate and faithful."[25] For Higginson, the significance of the Walden experiment was that it was an experiment in simple living and it allowed time to write what became a literary classic. His interpretation might be called the "bourgeois reduction of Thoreau": Thoreau as thrifty latter-day Puritan who follows what all sensible readers of his enduringly absorbing work will recognize as a legitimate and productive calling.

On the other hand, John Macy's *The Spirit of American Literature* (1913) sought to make Thoreau look appealing precisely because of his opposition to genteel norms. Macy seems to echo Higginson when he says "Thoreau does not, as some people imagine, argue the case for the wilderness against the town; on the contrary, he loves best the cultivated land with people in it. He merely uses the wilderness to try himself in." Macy's purpose in pulling Thoreau back into society, however, is not to legitimate him but to strengthen his credentials as a social radical, as "the one anarchist of great literary power in a nation of slavish conformity to legalism." Macy is the first American critic to put Thoreau's "Resistance to Civil Government" (popularly known as "Civil Disobedience") on the same plane of importance as *Walden*. He was very conscious of this innovation, noting impatiently, for example, that Thoreau's essays on "Wild Apples" and "The Succession of Forest Trees" had been school anthology pieces for a quarter of a century, whereas "the ringing revolt of the essay on 'Civil Disobedience' is still silenced under the thick respectability of our times." Macy praised *Walden* as Thoreau's "masterpiece," but as a social gospel rather than for its skill at representing nature, which he commends perfunctorily. Macy repeats Higginson's diagnosis in saying that Thoreau "merely uses the wilderness to try himself in," but to the end of marginalizing Thoreau's status as a nature writer and redefining him as a social critic.[26]

Thus the early twentieth century saw efforts both to rehabilitate Thoreau as a good mainstream American and to promote him as a radical dissenter. Often these two seemingly antithetical arguments coexisted innocently together, as in Bliss Perry's analysis of Thoreau's support for John Brown, quoted earlier. Macy, however, refused to play the juggler and pushed the image of a radical Thoreau further than any of his colleagues. This in itself is one sign that an author has achieved genuinely canonical status: when sharply differing codifications of literary history seek to claim him or her. Macy's appraisal is also notable as a foretaste of the next epoch in American Thoreau criticism. Higginson did nothing more than embroider on the original argument made by Emerson in his 1862 essay on Thoreau (with Lowell's, the significantly influential mid-century evaluation), that Thoreau was an exceptional naturist who had his crotchets yet remained a loyal American withal. Macy's position was not utterly original either; it was already current in radical circles.[27] Macy, however, was the first American literary historian not only to argue without apology the case for Thoreau's radicalism but also to locate "the spirit of American literature" in the quarrels of selected great figures with established American institutions. In this we see the origin of the so-called antinomian theory of American literature – the theory that the major American writers have been visionary dissenters – that came to dominate American scholarship between the 1920s and 1960s. This shift had a great deal to do with changing public impressions of who the great American writers were (thus Melville became canonized, Longfellow decanonized), of how to interpret their works (thus a Kafkaesque vision of Hawthorne superseded the earlier Jamesean vision of Hawthorne as urbane stylist), and which of their works seemed important (hence the rise of academic if not popular interest in Melville's most nihilistic work, *The Confidence-Man*).

Conclusion

Higginson's Thoreau typified the turn-of-the-century consensus that produced Thoreau's acceptance into the first American canon. In terms of that consensus, Thoreau gained in stature relative to 1860 because his eccentricities seemed trivial if not positively wholesome to this era of back-to-naturism, his books had measurable influence, the nature essay was more esteemed and widely practiced in America than during his own lifetime, and his obvious though indescribable excellence within that genre made him look more like Emerson's complement than his imitator – the Emerson connection now worked in favor of Thoreau rather than to his detriment. Bliss Perry showed a clear sense of the way the wind was blowing when he advised his boss that sales of Thoreau would enjoy a piggyback benefit from the Emerson centenary. The firm accordingly offered to distribute Emerson's 1862 essay on Thoreau as a pamphlet, free of charge, to anyone inquiring about purchase of the 1906 Thoreau edition. Nina Baym has argued that the first American canon was based on a vision not so much of the canonized writers as isolated individual geniuses, but as a kind of family group, a logic certainly applicable to how publishers and literary historians initially treated the Thoreau-Emerson link.[28] This close affiliation of the two Transcendentalist geniuses – first through biography and later through a combination of publisher monopoly and collective memory as shaped by a half-century of critical essays, literary histories, anthologies, advertisements, and other publisher manipulations – may indeed have been more important than any other factor in ensuring Thoreau's canonization at an earlier date than that of other American Renaissance figures now considered major who still languished in doubtful repute at the turn of the century.

Yet even as Thoreau won his place in the first American canon alongside the New England "big six" (Emerson, Hawthorne, Longfellow, Lowell, Holmes, and Whittier), a second canon that would displace it was in the process of being formed by Macy and others. To a greater degree than the first, this canon was based on a great-artist theory of literary history (the isolated genius, qualitatively different from the herd, who goes against the grain), a canon whose nineteenth-century heroes would include such figures as Edgar Allan Poe, Walt Whitman, and Mark Twain.

This newer vision was to have major consequences for how Thoreau was read. Macy's work shows this. His desire to promote Thoreau the nonconformist made him, for example, more hostile than gentleman-botanist Higginson to Thoreau's naturist bent, which worried Higginson only insofar as it might create a false impression of unsociability. Macy suspected that framing Thoreau as a literary naturist was a strategy of sanitization. As D. H. Lawrence remarked a decade later, "absolutely the safest thing to get your emotional reactions over is nature."[29] Indeed, had Macy read everything Higginson had ever written on Thoreau's behalf he might well have said "aha!" – because what clearly drew Higginson to Thoreau and what especially kept him there was the image of Thoreau the perceiver of beautiful unexpected microscopic truths about the flora and fauna of his own backyard. Macy would have been quick to perceive an alignment between the second, third, and fourth of the five turn-of-the-century justifications for elevating Thoreau: Thoreau the naturist, Thoreau as something loftier than mere nature writer, and Thoreau as good citizen. From a certain standpoint, these might all be taken as middle-class familiarizations of Thoreau.

What caused the gradual displacement of the first "genteel canon" by the idea of an "oppositional canon" is a question too complex to be fully explored here.[30] The change was quickened, on the one hand, by the emergence of an American radical intellectual establishment and, on the other, by the prestige of modernist experimentalism in literature and criticism, both of which took root toward the end of our period and set a high value on certain forms of dissenting expression: American traditions of protest for the former and a stylistic and conceptual individuality for the latter. In the long run, this reconception of the representative admirable American writer as a dissenting genius furthered the growth of Thoreau's prestige, although in the short run his acceptance into the first canon might have held him back. The most careful student of Thoreau's political reputation argues that Thoreau criticism until the late 1920s remained deadlocked in a redundant controversy over whether or not he was primarily a nature writer.

The autobiographies of two of the architects of the oppositional canon shed light on this problem. Van Wyck Brooks recalled being overdosed in youth with the nostalgic anecdotalism of a local schoolteacher who had had a sentimental friendship with H. G. O. Blake ("they walked together to Thoreau's grave and rowed on Walden pond, which was desecrated already by human innovation. For there were boat-houses on the beach and boats full of noisy girls profaned the spot where Thoreau had once embarked"). Young Brooks was forced to view Thoreau through a lens of prissy, fastidious respectability that must have reinforced his trenchant indictment of New England culture's thinness in *The Wine of the Puritans* (1909) and *Coming of Age in America* (1915). Not until the 1920s did Brooks take Thoreau seriously as a major, positive force in the history of American literature and thought, and then only because his interest was aroused by praise of Thoreau by Irish writer George Russell ("AE"), [31] for whom Thoreau had served as a model of cultural naturalism. Waldo Frank also came to think of Thoreau as America's first great writer only after long prejudice to the contrary. "When we were boys," reminisced Frank,

> we all had tedious uncles who professed to be very fond of Thoreau. They said that Thoreau was a great naturalist; that he wrote delightfully of butterflies and mushrooms. These uncles were typical good citizens of old America: altogether dull – mindless and sober paragons. We decided that their favorite author could be no favorite of ours. We took it for granted that Thoreau also was a stuffy bore.[32]

For the converted Frank, the "real" *Walden* is not the *Walden* of "Sounds" and "Brute Neighbors" but the *Walden* of "Economy."

That the image of Thoreau as literary nature-observer looked reactionary to Brooks and Frank does not mean that it was inherently so. It is striking that the late twentieth-century vision of Thoreau has begun to round back to the original one, but giving it a different spin. From the vantage point of the 1990s, when worldwide environmental concern has reached an all-time peak and is still growing, Thoreau's naturism looks more like a mode of dissent than it would have in 1910 to a radical critic gagging on repeated tributes to Thoreau the poet-naturalist. Indeed, even at that earlier moment the ideology of naturism was dividing, as the fledgling preservationist movement began to see as its adversaries not only the vested interests of industry but institutionalized conservationism as well. The founding genius of the Sierra Club, John Muir, in the light of such Thoreauvian dicta as "In wildness is the preservation of the world" (from "Walking"), began a promotion of Thoreau as the apostle of an absolute of wildness that in our time has taken a radical twist. Thus Earth First patron Edward Abbey ended his defense of the subversive potency of Thoreau's naturism by revising the conclusion to Emerson's eulogy: "wherever there is knowledge, wherever there is virtue, wherever there is beauty, he will find a home." Abbey's version reads: "Wherever there are deer and hawks, wherever there is liberty and danger, wherever there is wilderness, wherever there is a living river, Henry Thoreau will find his eternal home."[33] Emerson sought to gather Thoreau up into the higher reaches of moral idealism, an orthodoxy that Macy and Brooks had to break through. Abbey, however, reinterpreted the vision of Thoreau the inspirational man of nature as a counterestablishment stance.

What William Blake once wrote about Bible reading could easily be applied to the very different ways *Walden* has been read by early and recent admirers of Thoreau as literary naturist: "Both read the Bible day & night, / But thou readst black where I read white."[34] Barrett Wendell, perhaps the most sophisticated of the early literary historians, culminated his discussion of Thoreau by quoting the "well-known" last paragraph of the "Spring" chapter of *Walden* ("Early in May, the oaks, hickories, maples, and other trees . . . imparted a brightness like sunshine to the landscape") as a model of the "delicate sensitiveness" and precise grace in nature sketching that for Wendell was the essence of Thoreau's achievement in that book. Whereas Abbey, an even more admiring reader of *Walden,* chooses as *his* quotation from the end of "Spring" the portion of the previous paragraph where Thoreau mentions the "dead horse in the hollow by the path to my house" and "the assurance it gave me," despite the stink, "of the strong appetite and inviolable health of Nature" in its inexhaustible fecundity.[35] This for Abbey epitomizes Thoreau's consistently provocative stance in *Walden,* his practice of unsettling readers, contrary to Wendell's vision of a soothing, ingratiating style of descriptive prose. What has intervened between Wendell and Abbey is the concept of the oppositional canon.

In these two examples, the commentators' cultural frames have been crucial in determining their version of Thoreau. That is not to say they falsified him, simply that they saw his work through the filter of their respective images of literary excellence and American civilization. That is what canonization is all about – a culture's promotion of a figure or text to the status of a central reference point – and why it is important as part of our understanding of an author to take into account not only our own reactions to his or her work but the history of such readings, including – indeed, we might argue, especially – readings that dominated the thinking of what now seem bygone times. Through that effort we become more conscious of both the advantages and vulnerabilities of our own preferred angles of vision. It need not lessen the pleasure we gain from a text like *Walden* to make ourselves aware that our spontaneous interpretation is not inevitable, that it is bound by the limits of our cultural horizons. On the contrary, such awareness can bring with it an enriched sense of the text's possibilities, through its susceptibility to multiple repossessions, and an enriched sense of history, its many layers and strands that play through our languages and our lives, whether we realize it or not.

NOTES

1. Although challenges to the received canon have been especially vehement during the past two decades, canonical revisionism is hardly a new thing. See, for example, John Guillory, "The Ideology of Canon-Formation: T. S. Eliot and Cleanth Brooks," *Canons,* ed. Robert von Hallberg (Chicago and London: University of Chicago Press, 1984), pp. 337–62.
2. Chinua Achebe, "An Image of Africa," *Massachusetts Review* 18(1977), 788. Achebe modified this to "thoroughgoing racist" for reprinting in Robert Kimbrough, ed., *Heart of Darkness,* 3d ed. (New York and London: Norton, 1988), p. 257.
3. In Thoreau studies, three contributions I have found especially helpful are Walter Harding and Michael Meyer, *The New Thoreau Handbook* (New York: New York University Press, 1980), pp. 202–24; George

Hendrick and Fritz Oehlschlaeger, eds., *Toward the Making of Thoreau's Modern Reputation* (Urbana, Chicago, London: University of Illinois Press, 1979), pp. 1–54; and Michael Meyer, *Several More Lives to Live: Thoreau's Political Reputation in America* (Westport, Conn., and London: Greenwood Press, 1977).

4. *The Journal of Henry David Thoreau,* ed. Bradford Torrey and Francis H. Allen, 14 vols. (Boston and New York: Houghton Mifflin, 1906), vol. 5, p. 459. For Thoreau against commodification, see Michael T. Gilmore, "*Walden* and the 'Curse of Trade'," *American Romanticism in the Marketplace* (Chicago and London: University of Chicago Press, 1985), pp. 35–51. Stephen Fink's book-length study of Thoreau's professional career, *Prophet in the Marketplace* (Princeton: Princeton University Press, forthcoming), presents a more accommodating, pragmatic version of Thoreau, however.
5. Osgood Houghton, "Special Note to Postmasters," 1879, one-page printed circular, Houghton Mifflin collection, Houghton Library, Harvard University, MS Am 2030 (236). Here and at a number of points below I have drawn on this invaluable collection of printed and manuscript material; manuscript quotations are by permission of the Houghton Library.
6. George H. Mifflin, letter to A. F. Houghton and O. R. Houghton, April 8, 1903, quoted in Ellen Ballou, *The Building of the House: Houghton Mifflin's Formative Years* (Boston: Houghton Mifflin, 1970), p. 489.
7. See note 3 above, as well as Horace Hosmer, *Remembrances of Concord and the Thoreaus,* ed. George Hendrick (Urbana: University of Illinois Press, 1977) and Raymond Borst, *Henry David Thoreau: A Reference Guide, 1835–1899* (Boston: Hall, 1987).
8. *And Gladly Teach* (Boston and New York: Houghton Mifflin, 1935), pp. 185–6. In later life Perry reaffirmed that it was an uphill battle to persuade Houghton Mifflin to publish Thoreau's and Emerson's journals (manuscript letter to Francis Allen, June 7, 1950, Concord Free Library).
9. George H. Mifflin to Albert F. Houghton, April 6, 1903, typescript copy, Houghton Library, Harvard, MS Am 203 (189).
10. Bliss Perry, *The American Spirit in Literature* (New Haven: Yale University Press, 1921), pp. 130–1, 130, 131–2, 137.
11. George H. Mifflin to A. F. Houghton and O. A. Houghton, April 8, 1903, typescript copy, Houghton Library, Harvard, MS Am 203 (189).
12. Bliss Perry to E. H. Russell, April 9, 1903 and April 21, 1903, Houghton Library, Harvard, MS Am 2030 (217).
13. William P. Trent, *A History of American Literature, 1607–1765* (New

York: Appleton, 1903), p. 103; Barrett Wendell, *A Literary History of America* (New York: Scribner's, 1900), pp. 334–5.

14. Charles F. Richardson, *American Literature, 1607–1885* (New York and London: Putnam's, 1886), vol. 1, p. 388; Fred Lewis Pattee, *A History of American Literature* (New York, Boston, Chicago: Silver, Burdett, 1896), p. 225.
15. Houghton Mifflin 1895 brochure for "Standard Library Series," Houghton Library, Harvard, MS Am 2030 (242).
16. Houghton Mifflin promotional brochure, c. 1888, Houghton Library, Harvard, MS Am 2030 (238).
17. Ralph Waldo Emerson, "Thoreau," in *Complete Works of Ralph Waldo Emerson*, ed. Edward Waldo Emerson (Boston and New York: Houghton Mifflin, 1903–4), vol. 10, p. 459.
18. The first four quotations are from book notices culled from Houghton Mifflin scrapbooks and/or promotional brochures, Houghton Library, Harvard, MS Am 2030 (236, 242, 247, 248); the last is from an eight-page promotional piece advertising the 1906 edition of Thoreau's works, MS Am 2030 (246).
19. See Brooks's account in *Two Park Street: A Publishing Memoir* (Boston: Houghton Mifflin, 1986), pp. 154–7. Tersely modest, it nevertheless indicates the considerable significance of Brooks's role.
20. John Nichol, *American Literature: An Historical Sketch 1629–1880* (Edinburgh: Adam and Charles Black, 1882), p. 319; Julian Hawthorne and Leonard Lemmon, *American Literature: An Elementary Text-Book for Use in High Schools and Academies* (Boston: Heath, 1891), p. 150; John Beers, *An Outline Sketch of American Literature* (New York: Hunt & Easton, 1896), p. 144; Pattee, *A History of American Literature*, p. 227; Katherine Lee Bates, *American Literature* (Chautauqua: The Chautauqua Press, 1897), p. 265.
21. See especially Lynn L. Merrill, *The Romance of Victorian Natural History* (New York and Oxford: Oxford University Press, 1989).
22. Joseph Jackson, *Through Glade and Mead: A Contribution to Local Nature History* (Worcester, Mass.: Putnam Davis, 1894), pp. 18, 187.
23. F. O. Matthiessen, *American Renaissance* (London, New York, Toronto: Oxford University Press, 1941), pp. 166–75.
24. James Russell Lowell, "Thoreau," *North American Review* 101(1865), 597–608.
25. Thomas Wentworth Higginson and Henry Walcott Baynton, *A Reader's History of American Literature* (Boston, New York, Chicago: Houghton Mifflin, 1903), pp. 193, 195.
26. John Macy, *The Spirit of American Literature* (Garden City: Doubleday,

1913), pp. 183, 172, 173. For commentary on the significance of Macy's book, see Jay B. Hubbell, *Who Are the Major American Writers?* (Durham: Duke University Press, 1972), pp. 110–11; Richard Ruland, *The Rediscovery of American Literature* (Cambridge: Harvard University Press, 1967), p. 3; and especially Howard Mumford Jones, *The Theory of American Literature* (rev. ed., Ithaca: Cornell University Press, 1965), pp. 119–20.

27. Emma Goldman, *Anarchism and Other Essays* (New York: Mother Earth, 1917), p. 62. The essay appears to date from 1910. America's leading anarchist magazine *Liberty* called "Civil Disobedience" "an anarchist classic" as early as 1907 (vol. 16, no. 6, p. 1).
28. Nina Baym, "Early Histories of American Literature: A Chapter in the Institution of New England," *American Literary History*, 1(1989), 470–1.
29. D. H. Lawrence, *Studies in Classic American Literature* (1923; reprinted Garden City: Doubleday, 1951), p. 33. Lawrence would have chuckled at the following turn-of-the-century textbook endorsement: "No books can be put more securely into young hands than Thoreau's. Like Bryant, he should be read out of doors" [William Cranston Lawton, *Introduction to the Study of American Literature* (New York and Chicago: Globe, 1902), p. 143)].
30. The rise of what I am calling an oppositional canon, starting with Macy, is discussed in Jones, *The Theory of American Literature*, pp. 118–50. Gerald Graff connects this movement with the somewhat later rise of American literature as a scholarly profession, in *Professing Literature* (Chicago and London: University of Chicago Press, 1987), pp. 213–16. Thomas Bender's *New York Intellect* (Baltimore: Johns Hopkins University Press, 1987), pp. 206–62, is a valuable discussion of the turn from intellectual conservatism to radicalism. Chapter 1 of James Burkhart Gilbert, *Writers and Partisans: A History of Literary Radicalism in America* (New York, London, Sydney: John Wiley, 1968), pp. 8–47; Edward Abrahams, *The Lyrical Left and the Origins of Cultural Radicalism in America* (Charlottesville: University Press of Virginia, 1986), pp. 1–20; and Casey Nelson Blake, *Beloved Community* (Chapel Hill: University of North Caroline Press, 1990), shed light on the relationship between social and aesthetic radicalism during the prewar years.
31. Van Wyck Brooks, *An Autobiography* (New York: Dutton, 1965), pp. 47, 328–9.
32. Waldo Frank, *Our America* (New York: Boni and Liveright, 1919), pp. 151–2.

33. Emerson, "Thoreau," vol. 10, p. 485; Edward Abbey, "Down the River with Henry Thoreau," *Slumgullion Stew: An Edward Abbey Reader* (New York: Dutton, 1984), p. 307.
34. William Blake, "The Everlasting Gospel," final couplet, *Blake's Poetry and Designs,* ed. Mary Lynn Johnson and John. E. Grant (New York and London: Norton, 1979), p. 372.
35. Wendell, *A Literary History of America,* p. 335; Abbey, "Down the River," p. 289.

3

"Fishing in the Sky"

ANNE LABASTILLE

"I WOULD . . . fish in the sky, whose bottom is pebbly with stars."

One might imagine that Thoreau and I, and his writings, especially *Walden*, were meant for each other. I spent a childhood outdoors, early on determined to live alone in a cabin in the woods, and eventually did so. Thoreau *should* have been my instant idol, woods mentor, and beloved author. Not so.

I was to find that getting used to Thoreau and growing into *Walden* is an evolutionary process that may take half a lifetime. In my long conversion, I went from hating *Walden* and feeling cowed by it, to actually falling asleep over it, to starting to like and respect it, to ultimately imitating Thoreau's life-style, copying his cabin, and loving his book. Thus, when I was asked to write my responses to *Walden* as a woman, as a log cabin dweller, and an ecologist, I welcomed the opportunity.

As a college student in my twenties, confronted for the first time with reading *Walden*, I found it drudgery and shirked assignments. I never finished the book in class. My reasons were many. To begin with, Thoreau was fond of using Latin. I had suffered through two years of the language in private high school, but my small Latin was unequal to following him through. For instance, "patremfamilias bendacem, non emacem esse oportet" (p. 163). Halfway through his beautiful chapter on "Spring" I found "Eurus ad Auroram Nabathaeaque regna recessit" (p. 314), and was lost.

In addition, in his lofty way Thoreau often used very long sentences. Some careened along for sixty, seventy, and even one hundred words! In "Reading," for example, not recognizing Thoreau's satire, I stumbled through:

> They read the nine thousandth tale about Zebulon and Sophronia, and how they loved as none had ever loved before, and neither did the course of their true love run smooth, – at any rate, how it did run and stumble, and get up again and go on! how some poor unfortunate got up on a steeple, who had better never have gone up as far as the belfry; and then, having needlessly got him up there, the happy novelist rings the bell for all the world to come together and hear, O dear! how did he get down again! (p. 105)

Count them – one hundred and one words!

Still tiring the reader, Thoreau ends the next-to-last paragraph of *Walden* with this circuitous ninety-word sentence:

> Who knows what beautiful and winged life, whose egg has been buried for ages under many concentric layers of woodenness in the dead dry life of society, deposited at first in the alburnum of the green and living tree, which has been gradually converted into the semblance of its well-seasoned tomb – heard perchance gnawing out now for years by the astonished family of man, as they sat around the festive board, – may unexpectedly come forth from amidst society's most trivial and handselled furniture, to enjoy its perfect summer life at last! (p. 333)

Show me the college girl who would thrill to this.

There are many references in *Walden* to ancient books such as the *Gulistan, Harivansa, Vedas, Bhagvat Geeta,* and *Zendavestas.* These made me feel oppressed and self-conscious about how little I knew, how little I'd read. It was a task back then just to get through the *Norton Anthology of American Literature.*

Add to these complaints that I found certain chapters plain boring, such as "Reading," "Former Inhabitants," and "Winter Visitors." Some were hard going, as where Thoreau turns preachy and lets his schoolteacher self show through.

Worst of all was his poetry. There are about twenty verses in *Walden,* most composed by Henry David, as I shall call him herein with respect. I have long dabbled in free verse about nature, so scarcely warmed to rigid rhymes like this one from "Where I Lived, What I Lived For."

> There was a shepherd that did live,
> And held his thoughts as high
> As were the mounts whereon his flocks
> Did hourly feed him by. (p. 88)

And then there is his almost childlike ditty about the railroad.

> What's the railroad to me?
> I never go to see
> Where it ends.
> It fills a few hollows,
> And makes banks for the swallows,
> It sets the sand a-blowing,
> And the blackberries a-growing. (p. 22)

In short, I found most of Thoreau's poems pretty awful.

My outstanding experience from reading *Walden* in college was disillusionment. Later on, I came to realize that thousands of other readers have also felt this sense of betrayal. It stems from the fact that we imagined Thoreau lived his whole life in the woods as a sort of rugged Massachusetts pioneer. The subtitle of his book is *Life in the Woods.* When I discovered he only lived there two years, two months, and two days, and was situated only a mile from a neighbor, and grew beans, much of the glamor disappeared.

What my first phase with *Walden* came down to, then, was a poster on my dormitory wall at college that said, "We Need the Tonic of Wildness," and the fanciful vision of Thoreau surviving out in the woods for a short time. In the meanwhile, books like *White Fang, We Took to the Woods,* and *A Sand County Almanac* were more to my liking.

Not until my thirties, after a divorce and the purchase of twenty-two acres of wilderness land, did I try to read *Walden* again. Since I wished to build on my property, I trusted Thoreau's experience would help me construct a log cabin and live next to a lake with no road, as he had. I dutifully read a chapter each night, searching for clues and tips. But the book rambled so much, and touched on such a variety of subjects, that I usually fell asleep midway. I hadn't realized until then how much philosophy, as well as natural history, was hung on the framework of his two-year woods sojourn.

Henry Beston and *The Outermost House*[1] were actually the inspiration in fashioning my first log cabin, "West of the Wind," and in writing my first book, *Woodswoman.* He appealed to me because of his clear concise prose and strong nature images. I could see every window and board of his shack, smell the salt, hear the rolling combers in a storm. If he could write such a moving book about living a year on the great beach of Cape Cod, quite possibly I could build an Adirondack cabin, eke out a living there, and tell about it. If *The Outermost House* was the inspiration, a slim book entitled *The Wilderness Cabin*[2] was the carpentry manual. I pored over the pages, filled with sketches, plans, and measurements, until I'd chosen my own design, size, and materials. *Walden,* meantime, sat on a shelf.

My conversion to *Walden* began ten years later, as my mother lay dying in Miami. I made several long drives alone from the Adirondack Mountains of upstate New York to Florida. A friend suggested I listen to books-on-tape to help pass the miles. *Walden* was listed.[3] At last, I thought, I'll get through it without falling asleep or being bored; I and my two German shepherds would be a captive audience.

Whereas reading the book had always been hard work for me, the experience of hearing it was a revelation. Beautifully read, unabridged, with inflections, pauses, lilting tones, and expressive quotations, *Walden* suddenly flowed and flowered. Those sixteen hundred miles sped by as I listened spellbound for three days. I carefully rationed the twelve hours of tape, turning off my tape deck when traffic got heavy or the interstate circled cities. I never listened while snacking or after dark. Perhaps the pleasantly changing countryside added to my enjoyment and I believe that it helped increase my concentration. There was no work to *Walden* anymore. It was like hearing a charismatic professional actor on a huge, revolving stage. Years later, a scholar remarked on the irony of listening to one of the greatest nature writers and early ecologists on a tape deck at sixty-five miles per hour over the most heavily traveled highway east of California!

In my absorption, the first thing I noted were striking similarities between the way Thoreau had lived in his cabin, and how I was living in mine. Although he'd been but a couple of years in the woods and I ten, we came out the same on many matters. I especially loved his passages about being alone.

"I find it wholesome to be alone the greater part of the time. To be in company, even with the best, is soon wearisome and dissipating. I love to be alone. I never found the companion that was so companionable as solitude" (p. 135). And "I am no more lonely than the loon in the pond that laughs so loud, or than Walden Pond itself" (p. 137). Or "Why should I feel lonely? Is not our planet in the Milky Way?" (p. 133)

I also enjoy being alone at my cabin, "West of the Wind." I do confess to rare moments of discontent and loneliness. Living alone as a woman, perhaps I fear intruders (a rogue, robber, or rapist), or perhaps I am lovesick for a nonexistent, or distant, friend or sweetheart.

Thoreau, too, dealt with such a mood. He wrote

> I have never felt lonesome, – but once, and that was a few weeks after I came to the woods, when, for an hour, I doubted if the near neighborhood of man was not essential to a serene and healthy life. To be alone was something unpleasant. But I was at the same time conscious of a slight insanity in my mood, and seemed to foresee my recovery. . . . I was suddenly sensible of such sweet and beneficent society in Nature, in the very pattering of the drops, and in every sight and sound around my house, an infinite and unaccountable friendliness all at once like an atmosphere sustaining me. . . . Every little pine needle expanded and swelled with sympathy and befriended me. (p. 131)

We also had the common habit of early morning dips. Henry David writes "I got up early and bathed in the pond; that was a religious exercise, and one of the best things which I did" (p. 88). Also "in the forenoon, I usually bathed again in the pond, swimming across one of its coves for a stint, and washed the dust of labor from my person, or smoothed out the last wrinkle which study had made, and for the afternoon was absolutely free" (p. 167).

This is my pattern exactly. I embellish, however, with skinny-dipping whenever possible and sipping a strong espresso right after the chilly dawn dip. What did Thoreau wear? And drink besides water? Did he miss those swims as much as I do during the cold season?

Another compatibility I came upon is love of woodpiles. Says Thoreau, "Every man looks at his wood-pile with a kind of affection. I loved to have mine before my window, and the more chips the better to remind me of my pleasing work" (p. 251).

I'll go one step further and state that of all the hard work I do around the cabin, my favorite is cutting, splitting, and stacking firewood.

Both Henry David and I obtained drinking water from our lakes, after winter froze them, in precisely the same way and with the same appreciation.

> First I take an axe and pail, and go in search of water, . . . After a cold and snowy night it needed a divining-rod to find it. . . . I cut my way first through a foot of snow, and then a foot of ice, and open a window under my feet, where kneeling to drink, I look down into the quiet parlor of the fishes, pervaded by a softened light as through a window of ground glass . . . there a perennial waveless serenity reigns as in the amber twilight sky, . . . Heaven is under our feet as well as over our heads. (pp. 282–3)

I fell under the spell of *Walden* in my forties and it was Thoreau who inspired me to build a second tiny cabin twenty years after my first. Located on my land at an even more remote pond, the cabin was an attempt to withdraw from the increasing activity of summer vacationers, motorboats, and water-skiers on Black Bear Lake. I tried to copy Thoreau's cottage in whatever ways were feasible in spite of the isolated setting. I even named it "Thoreau II." This project led to my writing a sequel to *Woodswoman, Beyond Black Bear Lake,* describing this undertaking.

Now, in my early fifties, having built two cabins and lived in the woods over twenty years, I listen again to the *Walden* tapes as a way of preparing to write this chapter. Now I can easily pick up the book, browse a bit, and locate sections as familiar as old friends. Guess I've finally grown into *Walden.* More contemplative and well-read than my undergraduate self, I'm struck by the wide-ranging discourses of that wise young writer. Thoreau is like a trout fisherman, throwing out hook and bait, time after time. One cast is about economy; the next, solitude; the next, his bean field; then, winter animals. Behind each toss of the bait is the long, silvery, eloquent string of words, drawing the reader ever closer to the truth.

Let me now compare two cabin dwellers across the 140-odd-year span between us. When Thoreau took to the woods, he was considered eccentric by the townsfolk of Concord, Massachusetts. A few poets and scholars stopped by his house for thoughtful discussion, but by and large he stepped to that different drummer he wrote about.

When I moved into my first log cabin, I was to a great extent envied by summer people and year-round residents. Some of the locals considered me a nut, and still do. It seems that the urge to live alone in the woods is still not completely accepted, despite Earth Day, the "Greening of America," Grizzly Adams, and our collective national parks experience. My sense is that those masses of people in cities and towns who live "lives of quiet desperation" want everyone else to do so, too. Paradoxically, the more educated and well traveled a person is, the more he or she seems able to understand, empathize, and respect individuals choosing to live in isolation and close to nature. Also, since writing *Woodswoman* and *Beyond Black Bear Lake,* I am frequently asked by others, especially students and divorced women, how they, too, can build a cabin and get back to basics.

Imagine what my position and reputation, especially among women, would have been in 1845. A lone woman in pants and boots building her own house five miles from the nearest full-time neighbor and bathing in a mountain lake early each morning! It would have been almost impossible given the attitude toward women of those times – at least in Massachusetts.

My research into early (1700–1900) wilderness women has revealed that very few voluntarily lived alone in the woods, mountains, prairies, or deserts, despite the fact that we are a nation descended from pioneers and frontierfolk. Thousands went west in the company of their fathers, brothers, husbands, and lovers. In all my reading, I only encountered one female, Elinore Pruitt Stewart, a widowed laundress with a young daughter, who went to Wyoming to homestead – without a man – and loved living in the wilderness.[4]

In other respects, Thoreau's and my external conditions were quite alike. We built dwellings comparable in size. His was ten by fifteen feet; my first was twelve by eighteen feet, my second, ten by ten. Henry David began cutting and squaring his logs in late March, when he

> borrowed an axe and went down to the woods by Walden Pond, nearest to where I intended to build my house, and began to cut down some tall, arrowy white pines, still in their youth, for timbers. . . . So I went on for some days cutting and hewing timber, and also studs and rafters . . . singing to myself. . . . By the middle of April, my house was framed and ready for the raising. (pp. 40–2)

In my case, not wishing to cut a single tree on my wild forest tract, I contracted for timber to build my first cabin in 1965 with a lumber yard about fifteen miles away. They trucked forty-five red spruce logs (about 14 inches in diameter) to my lake and dumped them in after the ice went out in May. Making two trips, I towed them behind my old boat to the cabin site one and a half miles up the lake. Given the glacial speed of my motor with those enormous loads, it took two and a half hours. Securing the two log booms to shore, I started tonging and winching each timber up the slope, into the air, dropping it slowly into place on the mounting walls.

Henry David, in contrast, purchased an old shack from an Irishman, James Collins, for its wall and floor boards and one good window. His cost was $4.25. I paid $600 for my logs delivered (for my second cabin, the logs came from my land). When they were in place, they were walls indeed. I had to spend another $2,000 for materials like metal roofing, stoves, windows, flooring, and doors. There was no question at either abode of indoor plumbing, electricity, or telephone service. Thoreau dug a root cellar "in the side of a hill sloping south, where a woodchuck had formerly dug his burrow" (p. 44). I have a propane gas refrigerator. For heat, he had a brick fireplace and chimney; I, two wood stoves.

Both of us went to live on virgin land. "I am not aware that any man has ever built on the spot which I occupy," wrote Thoreau (p. 264). No one had ever lived on mine, nor pastured it, nor cut it, nor burned it, nor farmed it. By coincidence we also both took up residence on July 4th. The Walden cottage stood on eleven acres of private land which did not belong to Thoreau, but to Emerson, his older neighbor. I own twenty-two acres within the Adirondack Park, free and clear.

A few words of explanation will show the uniqueness of my locale. Recall that in 1845 there were no national or state parks in the United States, and very few, if any, refuges or sanctuaries for nature. America was still in an exploitative mode toward its natural resources and native residents. Therefore, the presence of the Adirondack Park makes my living situation decidedly different from that of Thoreau at Walden Pond.

The Adirondack Park is the largest (6 million acres) and second oldest (next to Yosemite) park preserve in the continental United States. Unlike Yosemite, which is a national park established in 1890, the Adirondacks are a state park created in 1892. They are a mix of "forever wild" state forest lands and private lands, roughly 40 percent and 60 percent, respectively. Within the state holdings, there are sixteen tracts of classified wilderness, totaling 1.1 million acres. I am fortunate to border one of these wilderness areas. From my window at "Thoreau II," I look across a pond toward fifty thousand acres where no motorized vehicles or float planes and no buildings are permitted. Only foot trails, tents, and songs in the air give evidence of humans here. This contrasts sharply with Henry David's situation. The Fitchburg Railroad was located sixteen hundred feet away across Walden Pond. A wagon road ran there as well, leading to the town of Concord about one and a half miles away.

The Adirondack Park is administered by two state agencies, the Department of Environmental Conservation (state lands) and the Adirondack Park Agency (private holdings). The park is free to anyone for recreation and enjoyment, but small fees are charged for use of state campsites and ski slopes. Most new buildings on private lands require a permit. There is no fee for the application form or permit itself, but there are the paper work, postage, and a long wait for processing.

I was required to get a permit for "Thoreau II," though it was classified as a rustic hunting-and-fishing cabin (under 100 square feet). I often thought how this process would have incensed Henry David and perhaps goaded him into another protest like "Civil Disobedience." He believed, as he wrote in "Civil Disobedience," "That government is best which governs not at all." In "The Village," he states: "I was never molested by any person but those who represented the state" (p. 72). If he had had to fill out Adirondack Park Agency forms, pay the postage back and forth, show his cabin site to a field officer, and pay ten dollars for a local building permit, I'm sure he would have felt "pursued and pawed with [men's] dirty institutions" (p. 71).

Certainly I chafed at the invasion of my woodland privacy and groaned over a seemingly silly piece of paper for a rustic trapper's shack with no road, no plumbing or septic system, and no utility lines, which I hoped no one but me would ever see. Nevertheless, my position was critically different. I have been a Commissioner of the Adirondack Park Agency for sixteen years and am sworn to protect the environmental quality of this great park. So although I personally grumbled, professionally I obeyed the law. I believe in conserving wilderness, wildlife, and wildlands with all my heart, and know of no other place in America that has achieved such wise regional land use plans. Thus, Henry and I took opposite positions regarding state intervention. He went to jail for not paying a poll tax. I dotted every i and crossed every t and paid every dollar before building "Thoreau II."

I kept a tally of my expenses for "Thoreau II" as Thoreau would have listed them. Thoreau's list reads:

> The exact cost of my house, paying the usual price for such materials as I used, but not counting the work, all of which was done by myself,[5] was as follows:

Boards	$8.03½,	mostly shanty boards
Refuse shingles for roof and sides	4.00	
Laths	1.25	
Two second-hand windows with glass	2.43	
One thousand old brick	4.00	
Two casks of lime	2.40	That was high.
Hair	0.31	More than I needed.
Mantle-tree iron	0.15	
Nails	3.90	
Hinges and screws	0.14	
Latch	0.10	
Chalk	0.01	
Transportation	1.40	I carried a good part on my back.
In all	$28.12½	

> These are all the materials, excepting the timber, stones, and sand, which I claimed by squatter's right. (pp. 48–9)

I also did a lot of the work on both cabins myself, but with "Thoreau II" I used "pioneer parties" of working friends on weekends to help cut and drag logs out of the woods surrounding the smaller structure. My costs were as follows:

17 one-by-eight-inch boards (scrounged from construction site)	$ 0.00
12 particle board sheets (scrounged from construction site)	0.00
Plastic sheeting	3.99
4 second-hand glass windows (given by neighbors)	0.00
2 second-hand doors (from neighbors)	0.00
4 firebricks for stove (from Rodney)	0.00
1 potbellied stove (from Mary)	0.00
Stovepipes, damper, cap	26.82
Asbestos wallboard (left over from #1 cabin)	0.00
Nails and spikes	9.76
Four 2 x 4s, and four 2 x 1s lumber	12.04
Hinges, hasp, padlock, hook for door	10.21
1 roll fiberglass insulation (for chinking)	12.77
1 chainsaw file	1.79
Steel roofing sheets (from dump)	0.00
1 kerosene lamp (to copy Thoreau's japanned lamp)	3.99
1 tin pail	2.89
1 small sink (from trash pile in Miami)	0.00
10′ sink pipe, drain with plastic connector, ring	8.12
Roof paint	4.88
Transportation (I carried everything on my back and in canoe)	0.00
Oil, kerosene, chainsaw gas	10.00
State taxes on materials (7%)	7.77
Local building permit	10.00
Adirondack Park Agency permit (postage only)	2.00
TOTAL	$130.75

Comparing \$28.12½ with \$130.75 isn't bad given the rate of inflation between 1845 and 1985!

Our cabins were furnished with Spartan simplicity. Thoreau's house and "Thoreau II" are almost identical. There are a desk, three chairs, a cup, a three-inch mirror, a pair of tongs and a dipper, a kettle and a skillet, silverware, and a kerosene lamp. Instead of using a bed as Henry did, I sleep on a mat in the tiny loft.

"West of the Wind," on the other hand, which is slightly larger and my permanent home, is more comfortably appointed with rugs, curtains, rocking chair, and two desks. It has a small gas-operated kitchen and lamps. Hundreds of books line my walls, whereas Thoreau probably kept his few on the table. Henry David apparently cooked outdoors as I do at "Thoreau II." He used his brick fireplace in inclement weather when he didn't walk home to his parents for dinner.

Henry's method of housework was novel.

> When my floor was dirty, I rose early, and, setting all of my furniture out of doors on the grass, . . . dashed water on the floor, and sprinkled white sand from the pond on it, and then with a broom scrubbed it clean and white; . . . and by [breakfast] the morning sun had dried my house sufficiently to allow me to move in again. (pp. 112–13)

I'm afraid that wouldn't work too well on my Navajo rugs in February. A stout broom, dust pan, and hand-pushed carpet sweeper do the job year-round.

The sounds that Thoreau described right around his house were a wonderful mix of the wild and the civilized. He speaks of wild pigeons, the whistle of the locomotive, church bells, cows, whip-poorwills, screech owls, the rumbling of wagons, frogs, baying dogs, squirrels, sturdy pines rubbing against the shingles, and a laughing loon.

At my cabin I hear frogs, barred owls, geese, squirrels, and soughing trees. These wild noises, however, are often drowned by the noisy technology of gas engines. There are A-10s, F-16s, motorboats, chain saws, seaplanes, log splitters, the rare lawn mower and ATV, the distant shrill of a fire engine on a south wind, distant commercial jets, and generators. Silence, that intangible natural resource, is getting hard to find, even in the Adirondack Park. But, thank God, there are still laughing loons.

Thoreau went to Walden, as we know, to "transact some private business with the fewest obstacles" (pp. 19–20), "to live deliberately, to front only the essential facts of life, and see if I could not learn what it had to teach" (p. 90). He wished to write what became *A Week on the Concord and Merrimack Rivers* and to take notes on his life in the woods.

Those were not my reasons. I went to Black Bear Lake in 1965 initially to be close to wilderness, observe wildlife, and become a writer. I had no idea what I would write, having been trained in wildlife ecology. I had a deeper drive as well, expressed best by Thomas Merton: "I live in the woods as a reminder that I am free not to be a number. There is, in fact, a choice."[6]

By the time I started building "Thoreau II" in 1985, my goals were well focused. Like Thoreau, I wished to write a specific book, to escape the growing summertime bustle, and to contemplate nature. By the 1980s this was getting harder and harder to do. In the 1960s, the Adirondack Park was not high on people's lists of places to go. Those who came had old family cottages on the lakes, or kids in local camps, or were working summer jobs to get through college, or loved trout fishing and big game hunting. I can recall how infrequently a boat went by my cabin. The sport snowmobile had yet to reach the mass market; I saw the first one speed by my homestead in 1971.

In the 1970s, patterns changed. The park opened up as a mecca for outdoor enthusiasts following the Earth Day movement. Snowmobiling as a winter sport mushroomed. Cabin fever disappeared. Then, as environment and ecology became household words and concerns in the eighties, even more folk came to the park in all seasons. Outdoor workshops, youth conservation corps, birdwatching groups, visitor interpretive centers, and college field classes proliferated. Late in the eighties real estate boomed here and everyone wanted a place on a lake. The number of vacation homes and summer visitors has probably more than tripled in the twenty-five years I've been in the park.

Paradoxically, like Henry, "I had more visitors while I lived at . . . " Walden/Black Bear . . . "than at any other time in Life" (pp. 143–4).

In addition to his unexpected visitors, Thoreau seemed to seek out people. He made almost daily walks to town and had frequent chats with ice cutters and railroad crews. There were many others such as fishermen, woodchoppers, waterfowl hunters, drivers of teams and sleighs, even poets. He spoke with them all. Says Henry David, "I am naturally no hermit" (p. 140).

Yet he did hold his solo afternoon walks precious, writing in his *Journal,* "The wood-path and the boat are my studio, where I maintain a sacred solitude and cannot admit promiscuous company . . . do not ask me for my afternoons."[7]

Since I travel widely and often on writing assignments, consulting trips, and lectures, my limited days at my cabins are as precious to me as Thoreau's afternoons were to him. I deliberately avoid people so that I may write and work more. Pals don't drop in for coffee. When I wish, however, I can and do mingle with summer folk, the mailboat driver, our lake's Fish and Game Club members. Or I can take my boat and truck and go the twelve bumpy miles to the closest hamlet and post office.

Two further differences struck me about our life-styles. Thoreau declared that, "by working about six weeks in a year, I could meet all the expenses of living. . . . For more than five years I maintained myself thus solely by the labor of my hands" (p. 69).

I find myself working constantly. I take no vacations and put in more hours than the average white collar professional. There seems no way I can let up and loaf. The exigencies of modern monetary demands are too harsh. Henry did not have to worry about insurance policies to cover a car, home, personal property, liability, accidents, and fires. He did not have Blue Cross or Blue Shield. He may have balked at paying a poll tax, but he surely wasn't bothered by land taxes, school taxes, state, county and city taxes, gasoline taxes, liquor and cigarette taxes, special taxes on new vehicles, and on and on.

I grow quite envious every time I read about Thoreau's summer mornings.

> Sometimes, . . . having taken my accustomed bath, I sat in my sunny doorway from sunrise till noon, rapt in a revery, amidst the pines and hickories and sumachs, in undisturbed solitude and stillness, while the birds sang around or flitted noiseless through the house, until by the sun falling in at my west window, or the noise of some traveller's wagon on the distant highway, I was reminded of the lapse of time. (p. 111)

Another irksome passage is Henry's contention about the postal service. "For my part," says he, "I could easily do without the post-office. I think that there are very few important communications made through it. To speak critically, I never received more than one or two letters in my life – I wrote this some years ago – that were worth the postage" (p. 94).

Imaginc, if you will, how strongly linked my work is with the post office. I live for the mail and by the mail. In summer, I faithfully meet the mailboat which delivers it to my dock. In fall and spring, I take my boat to the end of Black Bear Lake to connect with the mail truck. In winter, there is no delivery at all. I must trek out over the frozen lake. Sometimes, after rains, or near freeze-up and break-up, there are treacherous conditions. Sometimes the wind chill factor is thirty degrees Fahrenheit below zero. Once across the lake, I drive twelve miles over snowy roads to the post office. I still go because mail brings: checks, bills, manuscripts to be corrected, notices of dentist appointments, transactions of environmental conferences, letters from loved ones, wicks for my gas lamps, medicines, face cream, dog tags, chains for my saw, plugs for my outboard motor . . . Oh, Henry, where would I be without the post office?

As a woman, I am not at all touched by *Walden*. It reads as if Thoreau disregarded half the world's population. He barely mentions women. There is the odd reference to "Squaw Walden," to a ruddy and lusty old dame with an herb garden, to a poor black woman, and to the "Walden nymphs." There is slightly more about John Field's wife, who "was brave to cook so many successive dinners in the recesses of that lofty stove; with round greasy face and bare breast, still thinking to improve her condition one day; with the never absent mop in one hand, and yet no effects of it visible anywhere" (p. 204).

The day he left John Field's shack and ran down the hill, listening to his Good Genius, Thoreau probably never suspected a woman would thrill to his credo, that she would strive to make it her own, and to build and live in the woods, greatly and lately influenced by his example. This was his advice: "Go fish and hunt far and wide day by day, – farther and wider – and rest thee by many brooks and hearth-sides without misgiving. – Rise free from care before dawn, and seek adventures. Let the noon find thee by other lakes, and the night overtake thee everywhere at home. Grow wild according to thy nature" (p. 207).

I don't sense that Thoreau omitted women because he was a misogynist. Rather, that he was painfully shy and had little experience with women.[8] (It is interesting to note that none of the four Thoreau children ever married.) Perhaps if Thoreau had been more sympathetic to women, he would have been a more pleasing and supportive role model for me. In *Walden* he did not come across as a warm personality, but rather as a cold idol. I never felt he could be a hero, or that he needed mothering, or that I could imagine him as a kind of platonic, unthreatening lover. There was a chasteness, a purity about him. I sensed an intensely intellectual, precise, withdrawn, sometimes cynical man. I think he was selfish. In fact, he says as much in his chapter on "Philanthropy." "But all this is very selfish, . . . I confess that I have hitherto indulged very little in philanthropic enterprises" (p. 72).

Thoreau hardly seems the type who'd respond to a 911 emergency call or show up on a volunteer ambulance squad. No, I don't think Henry and I would have fallen for each other.

As an ecologist my reaction to Thoreau is far more positive. He was, in my opinion, one of the first prominent American ecologists. On January 1, 1858, he used the word ecology in a letter describing his friend Sam Hoar. Thoreau exhibited deep understanding and detailed knowledge of natural history and the interrelationship of species.

Fishing as he did, summer and winter, he described the food chain and trophic levels in "The Pond in Winter." It is classic ecology. Speaking of ice fishermen:

> [he] lays open logs to their core with his axe [searching for insects] . . . Such a man has some right to fish, and I love to see Nature carried out in him. The perch swallows thc grub-worm, the pickeral [*sic*] swallows the perch, and the fisherman swallows the pickeral; and so all the chinks in the scale of being are filled. (pp. 283–4)

As a Transcendentalist, he went on to consider "vast and cosmogonal themes in other spheres" while fishing for pouts under the stars. He wrote, "It seemed as if I might next cast my line upward . . . as well as downward. . . . Thus I caught two fishes as it were with one hook" (p. 175).

I'm glad Henry David is not here today to note the ravages of acid rain on fish and forests in certain parts of the country. Loving "God's Drops" so much, he would have been devastated to see the changes in his ponds. Thoreau's most eloquent chapter, at least for an ecologist, is "The Ponds." He took twenty-seven pages (pp. 173–200) to describe five ponds around his cabin. Calling them "Lakes of Light" – "gems of the woods" – "sky water," he packs those pages with wonderful aesthetic and ecological prose.

"A lake is the landscape's most beautiful and expressive feature. It is earth's eye. . . . Nothing so fair, so pure, and at the same time so large, as a lake, perchance, lies on the surface of the earth" (pp. 186, 188).

Some of Thoreau's favored ponds were undoubtedly of glacial origin, without inlets or outlets, deep and clear, sparsely vegetated. They did not suffer from acid rain damage, judging from the various fishes, amphibians, mammals, and waterbirds he describes. However, the seeds of the pollution problem were sown in the mid-1800s with the expansion of the Industrial Revolution, and these kettle-hole lakes, with no means to flush themselves, would have been early victims. It would be interesting to compare the pHs of Walden, White, Flint, and Goose today and in his time.

I have a similar set of ponds around my cabin. Like those Thoreau visited, they beckon, intrigue, and delight me. My lakelets are like good friends each with its own personality. But acid rain has spoiled them. Mine contain almost no fish, no white water lilies, no frogs, no salamanders. The pH of Black Bear Lake runs around 4.5 to 5.0 during the summers, or 100 times more acid than was normal in the 1930s. Lake water has high levels of aluminum and mercury which have leached from the soil. Many of the virgin red spruce I tried so hard to protect on my land have died. The Adirondacks are perhaps the worst-hit part of our nation, due to the high elevations, heavy precipitation, thin acidic soils, and prevailing winds from the industrial Midwest. I understand Massachusetts is also troubled by acidic precipitation which has recently affected Quabin Reservoir. Acid rain is a problem of global proportions, although it does have solutions.

If he were still alive, Thoreau would understand the linkages between the burning of fossil fuels, air pollution, acidic precipitation, and what they kill in the ecosystem. He would find that he could not catch two fishes on one hook anymore. He would speak out.

Thoreau was a conservationist who practiced "Small is beautiful." He made minimum demands on the earth, and lived with great frugality. He was also enough of an environmentalist to have understood the concept of "Spaceship Earth." He knew nothing, of course, about global warming or nuclear winter, raging forest fires in the Amazon, or oil slicks in the Persian Gulf. Yet he divined the fragile link between atmosphere and animals, the lifeline to which all creatures cling. His vision was clear. Note his lines in "House Warming," "nor need we trouble ourselves to speculate how the human race may be at last destroyed. It would be easy to cut their threads any time with a little sharper blast from the north. We go on dating from Cold Fridays and Great Snows; but a little colder Friday, or greater snow would put a period to man's existence on the globe" (p. 254).

Thoreau said he "left the woods for as good a reason as I went there. Perhaps it seemed to me I had several more lives to live, and could not spare any more time for that one" (p. 323). Did he leave because he had finished writing *A Week* and had two years' worth of notes on woods life? Did he have something better to go to? Did he wish to travel more? Was he still disappointed and lonely from his unrequited love for Ellen Sewall?

Whatever the reasons, Henry David could not easily live several more lives at Walden, given the logistics of that century. Even with the railroad so close to his cabin, long-distance travel was difficult in 1845, news was hard to obtain, intelligent companions for discussions scarce. Thoreau's intellect no doubt yearned for stimulation. At Walden he was probably famished for it at times. He had to get back to town to reach for his other lives.

Why did Thoreau leave the woods and I have not? I can quickly travel out by car, train, or plane to almost anywhere on earth within twenty-four to thirty-six hours. If I cannot physically be elsewhere, satellite imagery and connections can bring me news via TV or telephone from any corner of the world. Such intelligence and stimulation I find necessary and regenerating from time to time.

Perhaps I explained it best in *Beyond Black Bear Lake.*

> I shall live deliberately in my beloved Adirondacks. It's the best possible place for me. Here is West of the Wind, from which I'll fight environmental battles, and Thoreau II, to which I'll retreat for solace. Here are the beavers I swim with, the white-throated sparrows that wake me at dawn, the barred owls hooting me to sleep. Here, too, are the black bears and red squirrels that the dogs love to chase up trees. . . . I know I can cope with environmental changes, personal intrusions, and professional demands as long as I have my pocket of privacy and peace.

We may never know why Thoreau forsook Walden. But never mind. His sojourn there, even for so short a space, left us this enduring insight: "that if one advances confidently in the direction of his dreams, and endeavors to live the life which he has imagined, he will meet with a success unexpected in common hours" (p. 323).

Well done, Henry David, you master fisher – naturalist – philosopher – ecologist – carpenter – farmer – environmentalist – and writer of *Walden.*

NOTES

1. Henry Beston, *The Outermost House* (New York: Viking Press, 1928).
2. C. Rutstrum, *The Wilderness Cabin* (New York: Macmillan, 1961).
3. Available from Recorded Books, P.O. Box 79, Charlotte Hall, Md. 20622 (800-638-1304). The cost is $16.50 for rent of eight tapes that play twelve hours, or $56.95 for purchase.
4. Elinore Pruitt Stewart, *Letters of a Woman Homesteader* (Lincoln: University of Nebraska Press, 1961).
5. Except: "in the beginning of May, with the help of some of my acquaintances, . . . I set up the frame of my house" (p. 45).

6. Thomas Merton, *A Thomas Merton Reader,* ed. Thomas P. McDowell (Garden City, N.Y.: Doubleday & Co., 1974), p. 431.
7. *The Journal of Henry D. Thoreau,* ed. Bradford Torrey and Francis H. Allen (Boston: Houghton Mifflin, 1906), vol. 12, p. 333 (Sept. 16, 1859).
8. In *A Week* (chapter "Wednesday") Thoreau mentions knowing a "restless and intelligent woman. . . . I met her with pleasure as a natural person who not a little provokes me, and I suppose is stimulated in turn by myself." His love for Ellen Sewall is documented. The evidence of other works and letters indicates he was able to interact with, and write about, women.

4

The Crosscurrents of *Walden*'s Pastoral

H. DANIEL PECK

PROFESSIONAL literary critics have begun to acknowledge what students have always known: *Walden* is a very difficult and elusive book that continuously challenges, even subverts, the process of reading it. One critic has gone so far as to call *Walden* "bottomless," finding it a virtual conspiracy against the reader, who inevitably sinks into its boggy depths.[1] As much as this response may reflect some contemporary readers' experiences of *Walden*, it is difficult to reconcile with the confident generalizations of earlier critics, for whom the book's meanings were recognizable and clear. When R. W. B. Lewis in 1955 said of Thoreau's Adamic theme, "This is what *Walden* is about,"[2] he spoke for a previous generation's confidence in the book's manifest themes and issues.

Today, a generation later, few critics would dare claim to know precisely what *Walden* is about. For some, the question seems beside the point – a preoccupation with the work's merely thematic elements. Yet interpreters like Lewis didn't read *Walden* innocently or ignore its complexity. They deepened our responses to the book by placing it in the rich context of cultural myth. Their work pointedly revised earlier biographical and historical treatments of Thoreau by showing just how complex was the writer's response to the cultural mythology of his day.

Nevertheless, I think contemporary critics are right in finding *Walden* a more problematical book than did many earlier commentators. Students' persistent complaints about the book's difficulty and elusiveness, its capacity to swallow them up in its complex rhetorical movements, are warranted and ought to be taken seriously. Yet "difficulty" is one thing, "bottomlessness" is another. In finding *Walden* an infinitely porous text, some contemporary critics have seemed to remove it from the possibility of interpretation altogether, thus making *Walden* a greater literary anomaly than it is, as if to say that other great and complex works are not also characterized by dense intertextuality. There are, I think, more productive ways to address the difficulty of *Walden* than to stand in trepidation before its "bottomlessness."

I have suggested recently that at least some of *Walden*'s slushy bottom gets firmer if we come to understand the book's difficulty not only as the result of Thoreau's own determined indeterminacy (which must always be allowed for), but also as the result of a complex set of crosscurrents. Specifically, I've argued that *Walden* trails within it elements of doubt and loss that appear enigmatically, through parable, within the book's larger and more overt agendas of reform and renewal.[3]

One part of *Walden* that reveals its crossing currents is the "Former Inhabitants" subchapter. The overt level of meaning in this part of the book is established by Thoreau's confident dismissal of his predecessors at the pond, all of whose experiments failed to endure: "[H]ow little does the memory of these human inhabitants enhance the beauty of the landscape! Again, perhaps, Nature will try, with me for a first settler, and my house raised last spring to be the oldest in the hamlet" (p. 264). Thoreau, it would appear, has brought these inhabitants to mind simply in order to dismiss them – thus clearing the way for his own true and enduring act of settlement. Yet, as I have argued, the stories Thoreau tells about these former inhabitants reveal in their language not dismissal but attachment; the "Former Inhabitants" subchapter of *Walden* ties Thoreau and his experiment to his predecessors, and points to *Walden*'s buried themes: the writer's attachment to the human community, and the sense of loss and failure he shares with that community.[4]

The stories of the former inhabitants' lives, as seen from this perspective, are parables of loss, and should be linked to other parables in the book that describe Thoreau's own losses, such as the famous passage about the lost hound, bay horse, and turtledove. Through such parables, Thoreau gives loss a place in *Walden* without allowing it a full narrative relation to the book's more dominant themes of reform and renewal. These parables often appear disjunctively in the text, creating a sense of discontinuity, or interruption. To follow the language of *Walden*'s prevailing imagery, they are the ripples and ruffles – the perturbations – that occur on Walden's smooth surface when one submerged current runs against another. In this way, loss and the possibility of failure are admitted, and contained, within Walden's idyllic setting. In a book all about presentness ("the nick of time" [p. 17]), the past and its failures thus make their presence felt even as they are contained within the framework of Thoreau's prospective and utopian purposes.

If what I am saying sounds familiar, this may be because the phenomena I am describing belong to a very old literary type to which *Walden* belongs – the pastoral. Not pastoral in its pure Theocritan or Virgilian forms – there are no sheep in Walden – but pastoral in the complex sense of the term that evolved during the past three centuries in Europe and America, and which took on especially poignant meaning in the nineteenth century when romanticism confronted the emergent forces of modern industrialism.

According to theorists writing in this period, pastoral is not so much a literary form as a state of mind, or mode of thought. This was the position advanced by Friedrich Schiller at the beginning of the nineteenth century, and stated with remarkable clarity in the twentieth century by William Empson. Pastoral, Empson said, is the "*process* of putting the complex into the simple."[5] Yet if its processual nature is a key aspect of modern conceptions of pastoral, another equally important aspect is highlighted by Empson's phrase, "putting . . . into." That is to say, pastoral is a process of *containment*, which, in Herbert Lindenberger's words, "defines itself . . . through the forces with which it sets up tensions."[6] Here it may be useful to quote more fully from Lindenberger, one of the most sensitive contemporary students of pastoralism:

> [Pastoral] takes the form of an isolated moment, a kind of island in time, and one which gains its meaning and intensity through the tensions it creates with the historical world; further, . . . it uses the devices of language to exhibit itself as achieved and triumphant; yet . . . the very self-consciousness of its language betrays its essential precariousness and ultimately forces it to give way to another

mode of reality; finally, . . . the reader maintains a shifting and often ambivalent attitude toward the idyllic moment and the speaker who gives voice to it.[7]

For Lindenberger, the quintessential example of romantic pastoral is Rousseau's island of St. Pierre on the Lac de Bienne, as described at the end of his *Confessions* and in the Fifth Reverie, to which Rousseau fled following "the persecution he experienced at Motiers when an angry crowd hurled stones at his window." Lindenberger generalizes Rousseau's island into a state of mind he calls an "island experience," whose joyful simplicity is always qualified by a sense of the experience's fragility and precariousness.[8]

This is to say, pastoral is a form defined by the forces it contains, and by the tensions it exhibits; its very existence is predicated on the world (of civilization, urbanity, or technology) against which it positions itself, and from which its character(s) have fled. Without the felt presence of these forces on the boundary of the pastoral setting, and their expression *in* that setting, we would not have pastoral at all but something else: utopia perhaps.

Like Empson, Lindenberger says little about American literature (he focuses on German and English romanticism), yet his definition applies remarkably well to a number of American works we generally associate with pastoralism. James Fenimore Cooper's *The Deerslayer* (1841), for example, is "a world by itself,"[9] set in the wilderness of pre-Revolutionary America. Yet its idyllic setting, which D. H. Lawrence said was perhaps "lovelier than any place created in language," is electrified by the dangers that implicitly threaten its isolation. Commenting on this quality, Edmund Wilson called *The Deerslayer* "a dream full of danger."[10] The novel was written during a period in Cooper's life when he felt beleaguered by what Lindenberger calls "the historical world" – the social and political excesses, as Cooper saw them, of Jacksonian democracy. Those forces are always lurking just beyond the temporal framework of the Glimmerglass, and are embodied within the setting as a potential threat by greedy and violent characters such as Thomas Hutter.

Another familiar example of pastoralism from American literature is Mark Twain's *Adventures of Huckleberry Finn*. If Cooper's "island experience" is defined essentially by a centralized, static setting – a lake called Glimmerglass – Twain's is defined instead by movement. The pastoralism of *Huckleberry Finn* is, quite literally, an island experience, with Huck and Jim on the raft together, usually in flight down the river from the corruption and violence they encounter at every point along the Mississippi shore. Cooper's pastoral is defined by stasis and Twain's by flight; both are idylls realized through contrast with the dangerous historical worlds that lie on their (temporal or spatial) borders. Thus, in America too there are, in Empson's terms, several different versions of pastoral – each dependent on the unique ways in which a given writer's sensibility and historical situation work to fill the paradigms of pastoral experience.

What version of pastoral do we find in *Walden?* Its setting on the shore of a small and beautiful body of water links it to Cooper's Glimmerglass. Yet, unlike the Glimmerglass, Walden Pond is not particularly remote, either temporally or geographically, from the historical world. Its proximity to that world (represented by Concord, Massachusetts) aligns it more closely with Huckleberry Finn's raft – never very far from "sivilzation." Here is the key phrase, from *Walden*'s initial sentence: "When I wrote the following pages, or rather the bulk of them, I lived alone, in the woods, *a mile from any neighbor*" (p. 3; emphasis added). "A mile from any neighbor" seems intended to emphasize the distance Thoreau has established between himself and Concord, in order that his experiment in living should succeed. Yet, as we consider the scale represented by a mile's distance, even in the mid-nineteenth century, we are reminded that the experiment takes place *only* a mile from Thoreau's neighbors. As Leo Marx has written, Walden is a "middle" landscape – between civilization and wilderness – and this is an essential aspect of its pastoralism.[11]

From the perspective of this essay, the most important implication of Walden's proximity to Concord is the sense of contingency the proximity establishes. The "Visitors" chapter confirms the ease and frequency with which Thoreau's neighbors make their visits to Walden; some, like the "[g]irls and boys and young women [who] looked in the pond . . . and improved their time" (p. 153), are receptive enough to Thoreau's purposes, though, like that of his friend Therien, their relation to the pond is superficial. Others, like the ice cutters in "The Pond in Winter," approach Walden with motives utterly hostile to Thoreau's pastoral intentions. They would, if they could, carry the very pond away in their "shriek-[ing]" locomotive (p. 295).

The locomotive, and the technology it represents, is the most immediate threat to Walden as a pastoral environment. It most obviously gives expression *in* that environment to the historical world, directly extending the influence of Concord, and of the whole world of communities the railroad links, to Walden.[12] The railroad has "infringed on [the Pond's] border" (p. 192), and its adjacency to Walden is made vivid in Thoreau's 1846 survey drawing of the pond (see Plate 1), a version of which was printed in *Walden*'s first edition. The only element in the drawing not directly related to the natural contours of the pond is a ruled line, drawn aslant, almost touching the southwest shoreline, labeled "Rail Road." This relation of adjacency symbolizes the entire set of contingent relations that, in *Walden,* Thoreau has established with the historical world.

Yet, as Thoreau's survey map suggests, these relations are both manifested *and* given context by adjacency. When Leo Marx considered the machine in Thoreau's (and American culture's) garden, he drew upon George Inness's painting "The Lackawanna Valley" (1855; see Plate 2), which shows a locomotive proceeding forward into the center of a landscape whose scattered stumps suggest the railroad's destructive force. In his brilliant analysis of this picture, Marx shows that, for all the centrality of the locomotive, the painting reconciles the technological and the agrarian through various pictorial means: softening the lines of industrial structures such as the railroad roundhouse, creating a visual relation between the locomotive's smoke and the natural mist of the atmosphere, and setting in classically pastoral pose a rural viewer reclining in the foreground. Marx compares these effects to Thoreau's description of the railroad's deep cut in *Walden,* where a technological image is transformed into an organic one.[13]

"Lackawanna Valley" suggests Inness's overt attempt to reconcile agrarian and technological elements; he was commissioned by the railroad company to paint this picture, and seems initially to

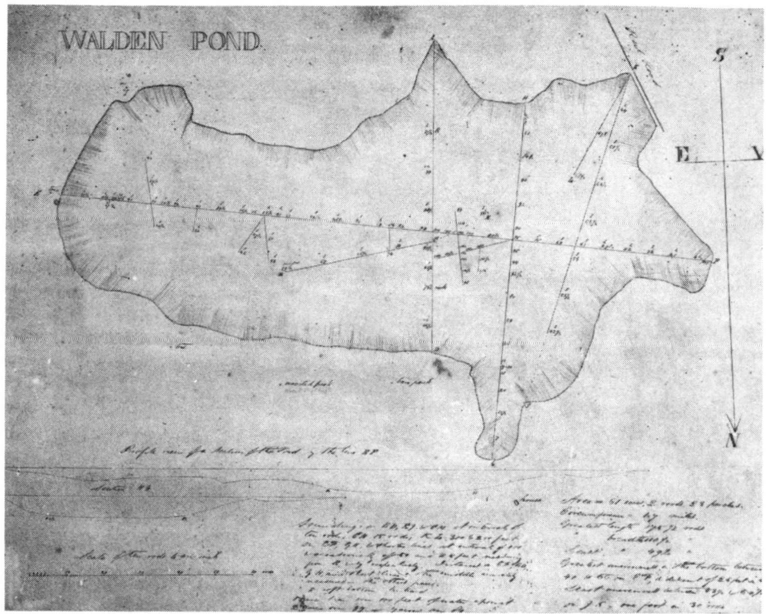

Plate 1. *Walden Pond Survey,* drawn by Henry David Thoreau. Concord Free Public Library.

have resisted the assignment – until he hit on the specific effects Marx regards as "ingenious."[14] In extending Marx's argument into an analysis of the overall composition of "Lackawanna Valley," we might observe that the upper and lower portions of the picture are visually quite distinct: The upper portion is filled with a gray monotonal sky, and the lower portion – which dominates the scene – depicts the locomotive and the hillside of stumps. The sectors exist in what might be called a vertical, and potentially oppositional, visual relation to one another.

The distinctness of the two realms suggests the need for reconciliation, which Inness achieves through the skillful use of discrete, thematic images whose essential purpose is mediation of the picture's polar elements. For example, the tall tree in the left foreground (the only live tree in this part of the picture) reaches dramatically from the lower realm to the higher, thus linking them and unmistakably presencing itself as a mediating element. Having

Plate 2. George Inness, *The Lackawanna Valley.* National Gallery of Art, Washington, D.C., gift of Mrs. Huttleston Rogers.

been charged with portraying technology – and thus of necessity foregrounding it (the locomotive advancing into the center of the scene) – Inness must address the machine and its already invested cultural meanings more or less directly. Thoreau's transformation of the railroad cut from an industrial to an organic image reflects just such a direct engagement with, and mediation of, the machine. We may also consider, in this context, his treatment of the ice cutting industry, whose potentially destructive work results, ironically, in Walden's water merging with that of the sacred Ganges. Both these examples dramatize one of *Walden*'s key pastoral strategies.

There is another, equally important, pastoral strategy in *Walden* to which neither "Lackawanna Valley" nor Marx's critique of it answers very well. This strategy I have called containment; it does its work less through direct mediation of particular elements than through an overarching composition. It achieves its effects *in*directly through *Walden*'s pervasive mode of adjacency or deflection. For a visual analogy to this structural mode of *Walden*'s pas-

Plate 3. George Inness, *On the Delaware River.* The Brooklyn Museum, Special Subscription Funds.

toralism, we may turn to another of Inness's paintings – "On the Delaware River," completed in the early 1860s (see Plate 3). The river, painted as a flow of water widening toward the viewer into something closely resembling a lake or pond, is seen with cattle grazing near the shoreline. In its broad horizontality, the picture's design tends to merge the upper and lower portions, which in any case are merged visually by their similar coloration and texture. The towering cumulus clouds, for example, reflect the brown tones of the hills below.[15]

As we view this picture, the eye is drawn to an area illuminated by sunlight and made radiant by lush green tones, in the left middle distance. Here, looking serenely out over the water, is a white cow, undisturbed by the nearby presence of an advancing locomotive. Unlike its counterpart in "Lackawanna Valley," this locomotive is not moving toward the center of the scene but is moving away from it; already on the periphery, it will soon be out of sight. The locomotive seems curiously miniaturized, diminished to a smaller scale than the landscape. Although the locomotive, rendered very small and partly hidden by foliage, seems almost incidental to Inness's larger scene of natural beauty, the line of railroad tracks extending ahead and behind the train forms a main compositional axis of the painting. It joins the line of the large hill in the right background, creating one of the picture's two major left-right diagonals, whose intersection forms a broad, flattened X.

This design also roughly describes "Lackawanna Valley," where lines of trees on both left and right extend the diagonals formed by the dividing railroad tracks. The difference is the striking integration of composition in "On the Delaware," so tightly symmetrical and so balanced that the railroad tracks are fully absorbed into the larger (pastoral) sense of the whole. The symmetry of "On the Delaware River" is analogous to the way in which *Walden*'s diverse currents of meaning are contained within the book's overarching seasonal structure. We may also think here of Thoreau's discovery of the intersection of the pond's width and length at exactly its deepest point, and, more broadly, of the phenomenon he calls "the equilibrium of the whole lake" (p. 187).

There is a locomotive in "On the Delaware River," but its presence is *structurally* contained by the painting's composition. Because of the structure, the locomotive seems no more threatening than do the boatmen in the same picture, whose barges float serenely with the river's current. As in *Walden*, the machine enters Inness's garden, but its force is deflected, literally marginalized. The power of industrialism is discharged through its oblique relationship, created by the artist, to the landscape's other features. Technology shows itself here, but its lines of force – as in Thoreau's map of Walden – are drawn aslant, deflected away from the pastoral center of the picture.

Viewed together, "Lackawanna Valley" and "On the Delaware River" can thus illuminate *Walden*'s shifting pastoral strategies. Yet both these pictures, through different means, achieve a serenity that is, finally, not characteristic of *Walden*. Unlike Inness's peaceful valley or the broad, reassuring currents of his Delaware, *Walden* never achieves resolution of its conflicts; it is always showing us its crosscurrents, its ripples and ruffles.[16] Some of the differences between *Walden* and Inness's paintings lie in the temporality that inexorably makes itself felt in narrative, in contrast to the spatiality (and resistance to temporality) visual art characteristically exhibits. More important, the greater complexity of *Walden*'s pastoralism is due to the fact that Thoreau never wants us to forget for very long about the historical world and how it might force its way across Walden's boundaries. The very firmness of *Walden*'s seasonal structure serves, in part, to hold back the force of time and history always threatening the pond's borders. Walden's geography, as Thoreau images it in "The Ponds" chapter, symbolizes this vulnerability:

> I have said that Walden has no *visible* inlet nor outlet, but it is on the one hand *distantly and indirectly* related to Flint's Pond, which is more elevated, by a chain of small ponds coming from that quarter, and on the other *directly and manifestly* to Concord River, which is lower, by a similar chain of ponds through which *in some other geological period it may have flowed, and by a little digging, which God forbid, it can be made to flow thither again.* If by living thus reserved and austere, like a hermit in the woods, so long, it has acquired such wonderful purity, who would not regret that the comparatively impure waters of Flint's Pond should be mingled with it, or itself should ever go to waste its sweetness in the ocean wave? (p. 194; emphases added)

The qualifier "visible" at the outset of this passage hints at the unstable, even illusory quality of Walden's protected isolation. Given what Thoreau says about the impure waters of Flint's Pond (and, indeed, about the greedy farmer who sullied the pond with his name), we can easily understand the nature of their "distant and indirect" threat to Walden's purity. Part of Thoreau's purpose in describing Flint's Pond is to image the possibility of Walden's spoliation. The more "direct and manifest" threat to Walden, however, as the passage makes clear, is its proximity to the Concord River. Only a "little digging" would return the pond to the river, which is to say, the river of time.

We know from Thoreau's earlier book, *A Week on the Concord and Merrimack Rivers* (1849), that for him the Concord River was deeply associated with New England's history of exploration and settlement – a history that is largely, as Thoreau recounts it in that book, one of destruction and spoliation.[17] God should "forbid" the remerging of Walden with the Concord because this would rob Walden of its identity. Though the pond is "*Walled-in*" (p. 183), as

Thoreau puns elsewhere in "The Ponds" chapter, it is in the very nature of *Walden*'s pastoralism that its boundaries are insecure and that the river of time runs so dangerously near.

All the key terms in the above passage make clear that Walden is an analogue for the self, and for the privileged and protected isolation Thoreau hopes to achieve at the pond. Another such analogue is the Hollowell farm, described in "Where I Lived, and What I Lived For":

> The real attractions of the Hollowell farm, to me, were; its *complete retirement, being about two miles from the village, half a mile from the nearest neighbor,* and *separated* from the highway by a broad field; its *bounding* on the river, which the owner said *protected* it by its fogs from frosts in the spring, though that was nothing to me; the gray color and ruinous state of the house and barn, and the dilapidated fences, which put such an *interval* between me and the last occupant; the hollow and lichen-covered apple trees, gnawed by rabbits, showing what kind of neighbors I should have; but above all, the recollection I had of it from my earliest voyages up the river, when the house was *concealed behind* a dense grove of red maples, through which I heard the house-dog bark. (p. 83; emphases added)

On the surface, this passage exemplifies Thoreau's Emersonian belief that the best form of ownership of the landscape is spiritual. Yet there are deeper levels of psychic activity in this anecdote, for securing the Hollowell farm is only the first step in a longer process. There remain the tasks of holding and protecting this imaginative space. These activities belong to a dimension of *Walden*'s pastoralism ignored by ideological readings such as Leo Marx's. They point to a phenomenon that Renato Poggioli calls "the pastoral of the self."[18]

The terms in the Hollowell Farm passage to which I have given emphasis all suggest boundary and protectedness, and the phrase "half a mile from the nearest neighbor" echoes Thoreau's own bounded situation at the pond. Yet in a "middle" landscape, boundaries are by nature permeable, and require a special act of consciousness to maintain. In part, this simply means holding the world off, resisting its influences, and many of the polemical sections of *Walden* work toward this end by describing the necessary discipline of solitude. As Thoreau says to "pilgrims" in the "Visitors" chapter, it is necessary to "really [leave] the village behind" (p. 154).

To *really* leave the village behind involves a process not only of walling out its influences, but also of walling in the experiences Walden affords – of articulating the world that lies inside the boundary. The particular kind of tension that defines *Walden*'s pastoralism has as much to do with Thoreau's desire to keep Concord and Walden apart as it does with the actual oppositional features of the settings. The boundary of Thoreau's Walden "yard" (p. 113), as he calls it (playing on images of domestic and civilized space), is drawn not only by holding off those forces that would cross his boundary, but also by sharply defining what lies inside the boundary, activities that occur with special intensity in the chapter "Brute Neighbors," where the radius of Thoreau's world (his arc of perception) is both circumscribed and filled to repletion. The elements of this "inside" space, according to the inevitable dynamic of pastoralism, contrast with everything that lies outside it. The point is that the contrast itself is a product of consciousness, and all Walden's various "bounds," "separations," and "intervals" are marked off and maintained by the pastoral imagination.

As I have commented elsewhere, this act of consciousness in *Walden* might be called "worlding" – a supremely creative act of imagination that establishes intimacy between Thoreau and his environment, giving to that environment a sense of pure immanence.[19] The whole of the long initial chapter, "Economy," may be regarded as preparation for this process: It describes the erection of a house and the rationale for having done so, for having positioned the self outside society, and laying the groundwork for the kind of pastoral experience such building may enable. As Heidegger writes, "We attain to dwelling . . . only by means of building."[20]

This process of "worlding" is by nature creative and visionary, and extends – ultimately transcends – the carpentry of Thoreau's hut building. As with his vision of the deep cut, Thoreau's larger pastoral vision of the pond is just that: a vision. Perhaps because we know that his experiment really happened we may fail to see that, as Cooper dreamed into being his Glimmerglass (a real place transformed, as Lawrence knew, by wish fulfillment),[21] Thoreau also dreamed his Walden into being. Though every detail in *Walden* may be "true," its world is brought to existence – willed there and sustained, "held" in place – by imagination. This act of holding a fragile and tenuous world in place is the essential work of *Walden*. It is not easy work, and it certainly cannot be sustained indefinitely. Though Thoreau "had several more lives to live" (p. 323), other commitments to keep, it is in the very nature of pastorals, as Lindenberger says, that they should end. They are temporal islands as well as spatial ones.

The pastoralism of *Walden* thus enacts a process (to reverse Frost's order in "Mending Wall") of walling out and walling in, of establishing boundaries against threats to the pond's integrity, and bringing the world that lies inside those boundaries luminously into focus. There is a further distinction to be made in defining Walden's pastoralism. Returning to the final portion of Thoreau's description of the Hollowell farm, we learn that of all the farm's advantages for him, the most important is the way it lies in his memory, the way his "recollection" holds it there. In that recollection, the farm is "concealed behind" a grove of maples, a concealment symbolic of the way memory guards Thoreau's childhood vision, keeping it safe (in private experience, in reverie) from the historical world. The Hollowell farm, as seen in this vision, is cognate with Thoreau's childhood memory of Walden Pond, "that fabulous landscape of [his] infant dreams" (p. 156).

In Thoreau's world and, indeed, in all our worlds, memory carries pain as well as reverie. He could not have "recollected" his "earliest voyages up the river" without recalling the brother who died tragically, and with whom he had made the most memorable of such voyages (recounted in *A Week*). To recollect experience in narrative form is necessarily to filter it – to focus on some aspect of the past, and, in so doing, exclude some other aspect.

"Recollecting" always involves the risk of opening the floodgates of memory, with all the pain and loss they hold back, and in this risk lie the deepest purposes of "concealment." One of the most interesting aspects of *A Week* is its complex negotiation between gain and loss, reverie and pain, as the river carries Thoreau deep into New England's and his own past. Written partly as an elegy to his brother, *A Week*'s most obvious gesture of (self)concealment is the writer's refusal (inability?) to use his brother's name. In many other, more subtle ways as well, *A Week* conceals and reveals according to the dictates of its own version of experience.

One of the things, then, that *Walden* as a pastoral excludes from its world is other versions of Thoreau's life – including the version told in *A Week*. Thanks to modern scholars, we now know how contemporaneous was the composition of these two works, their initial versions proceeding side by side at the pond, each reflecting different sides of the same life.[22] The essential way in which *A Week* engages the historical world is through immersion in the river of time – the voyager witnessing the world's manifestations along the shores of two rivers, and ultimately merging the two into one river of the imagination. In *Walden,* on the other hand, the rivering (progressive) mode gives way to the mode of pastoral retreat into a static setting: "my yard" (p. 271). Excluded from this yard is not only the historical world, but also the self's other approaches to that world.

Among those approaches is the one taken in Thoreau's *Journal.* This vast document, overarching both *A Week* and *Walden* during the twenty-four years of its composition (1837–1861), is an essentially private and meditative text. Where *A Week* and *Walden,* for all their stylistic and structural idiosyncrasies, strive for closure and resolution, the *Journal* is an endlessly provisional document, in which one day's observation might be superseded by that of the next. In this context, doubts, ambiguities, and uncertainties could be openly entertained. Consider, for example, the following *Journal* passage written in January 1852, several years after Thoreau had left the pond but two and a half years before the publication of *Walden:*

> But why I changed? why I left the woods? I do not think that I can tell. I have often wished myself back. I do not know any better how I ever came to go there. . . . Perhaps I wanted a change. There was a little stagnation, it may be. About 2 o'clock in the afternoon the

> world's axle creaked as if it needed greasing. . . . Perhaps if I lived there much longer, I might live there forever. One would think twice before he accepted heaven on such terms.[23]

This *Journal* passage challenges the "deliberateness" of the Walden experiment's beginning and end ("I had several more lives to live"), as they are recounted in *Walden.* It would be a mistake to conclude, however, that the *Journal* gives the true account of the Walden years and that *Walden* gives an artful version. Both accounts are "versions" and, indeed, the *Journal*'s account is expressed in its own, distinctive form of (meditative) art. By 1850, Thoreau unmistakably considered his journal-keeping an integral mode of writing, which he assiduously and "deliberately" practiced for the rest of his life. The point of putting this *Journal* passage against *Walden* is not to reveal the fictitious nature of *Walden*'s rendering, but to underscore the way in which it excludes other versions of the writer's experience. In this case, the version excluded is one that – more than *Walden* – takes account of the historical world, and, in doing so, questions the enduring value of the pastoral life ("One would think twice before he accepted heaven on such terms").

Similarly, the confrontation with nature's "wildness," its frightening otherness, that Thoreau describes in both *The Maine Woods* (especially in "Ktaadn") and *Cape Cod* are largely excluded from consideration in *Walden.* Such exclusions are never absolute, however. No more than the locomotive's shriek can be silenced at Walden can the self's other versions of experience be barred. They will break through, often obliquely in the form of parable – as in the stories of failure, devastation, and death recounted in "Former Inhabitants." These stories make the same point about pastoral experience as does Nicolas Poussin's famous painting, "Et in Arcadia Ego": Even in Walden we find the presence of death, and all the issuances of failure and loss that death implies.

Among *Walden*'s various chapters and subchapters, "Former Inhabitants" provides perhaps the most open view of the book's complex crosscurrents. Yet in the very nature of *Walden* as a pastoral the perturbations caused by the historical world are always implicitly present, and observable, even in the book's most idyllic moment. By most accounts, that moment occurs in the central chapter, "The Ponds," which renders a sustained, lyrical description of Walden's beauty and "crystalline purity" (p. 177). This chapter is preceded by "The Village," but the apparent contrast between the two chapters is less significant than their titles suggest. "The Village" is less about Concord than it is about Thoreau's new orientation toward it. So fully relocated (at the pond) is his perspective by this point in *Walden* that he now sees the village with the clarity of distance, almost as an anthropologist might; all Concord's essential shapes and functions become apparent to him. Thoreau's "dreaming" (p. 170), instinctual return to his hut at the conclusion of this chapter shows how fully he has adopted the pastoral perspective toward experience.

Thus, as we enter "The Ponds" chapter we are well prepared for the extended description of Walden's timeless "lines of beauty" (p. 188). Thoreau's celebration of the pond's purity and (spiritual) light sustains itself for seven full pages and culminates in his exclamation, "How peaceful the phenomena of the lake!"; Walden, he says at this point, is "a perfect forest mirror" (p. 188). But following Thoreau's reiteration of the pond's "remarkably smooth" surface, and his assertion that in November there is "absolutely nothing to ripple [it]" (p. 189), we suddenly sense a ripple forming – a shift away from the pure spatiality of landscape description and toward the historical world.

The shift is introduced, as we might expect, by a remembrance – one expressed in a distinctively pastoral mode. Thoreau consults an "old man," who "remembers" for him an earlier Walden of greater plenitude. This consultation prompts Thoreau's memory of his own past at the pond ("when I first looked into these depths"; "when I first paddled a boat on Walden" [p. 191]), which at first leads him even deeper into reverie: "I have spent many an hour, when I was younger, floating over [Walden's] surface as the zephyr willed, having paddled my boat to the middle, and lying on my back across the seats, in a summer forenoon, dreaming awake" (p. 191). Soon, however, remembrance leads Thoreau in quite another direction. With surprising rapidity, the passage turns to loss; indeed, it becomes a virtual declension of loss.

> But since I left those shores the woodchoppers have still further laid them waste, and now for many a year there will be no more ram-

bling through the aisles of the woods, with occasional vistas through which you see the water. My Muse may be excused if she is silent henceforth. How can you expect the birds to sing when their groves are cut down?

Now the trunks of trees on the bottom, and the old log canoe, and the dark surrounding woods, are gone, and the villagers, who scarcely know where it lies, instead of going to the pond to bathe or drink, are thinking to bring its water, which should be as sacred as the Ganges at least, to the village in a pipe, to wash their dishes with! – to earn their Walden by the turning of a cock or drawing of a plug! That devilish Iron Horse, whose ear-rending neigh is heard throughout the town, has muddied the Boiling Spring with his foot, and he it is that has browsed off all the woods on Walden shore; that Trojan horse, with a thousand men in his belly, introduced by mercenary Greeks! Where is the country's champion, the Moore of Moore Hall, to meet him at the Deep Cut and thrust an avenging lance between the ribs of the bloated pest?

Nevertheless, of all the characters I have known, perhaps Walden wears best, and best preserves its purity. (p. 192)

I have quoted this passage at length to remind the reader how sustained is Thoreau's sense of loss in this section of "The Ponds," how sharply the passage contrasts with what immediately precedes it, and how that loss leads him ultimately to anger. As we weigh these accumulated losses and sense the intensity of Thoreau's building anger toward the historical world (focused by, but not limited to, the railroad), we may be struck by how much work the word that begins the final quoted sentence must do. "Nevertheless"?! How much this mere transition must clear away to restore the sense of Walden's "purity," stated at the sentence's end. Of course, the word does no real work at all, neither confronting nor rationalizing loss but simply pushing it aside.

"Nevertheless" is a verbal gesture of a distinctively pastoral kind. Rather than directly engaging the realities it displaces, it deflects them, turns them aslant. Its purpose is to smooth the temporarily ruffled surface of the pond, to right the balance of the pastoral mode, to restore the idyll that was interrupted, an interruption that came from Thoreau himself, from his historical memory, which contains both reverie and loss. These are the different "versions" of experience that are always competing with one another in *Walden,* resulting in the peculiar tension that defines its pastoralism.

As we turn back to the earlier, idyllic portion of "The Ponds," viewing it in light of this interruption, we notice that Thoreau explicitly identifies the chapter's visualization of the pond as belonging to the year 1852 (p. 180) – long after the Walden experiment (1845–46), and very late in the book's composition. This observation reminds us of how synthetic a book *Walden* is. Long ago J. Lyndon Shanley discovered the extraordinary fact that *Walden* was written in at least seven separate versions, over a period of almost a decade.[24] Each of these versions (and, indeed, many discrete elements within them) may be understood as a version of the Thoreauvian self, each telling its own story from a different time and perspective and finding its own relation (not always comfortably) to the book's many other stories.[25]

But the essential story of *Walden,* as Sherman Paul has written, is one of joy and self-renewal;[26] his book, Thoreau asserts early in the narrative, will not be "an ode to dejection" (p. 84). This insistent disclaimer, we may say, provides the fundamental "control" of *Walden*'s pastoralism. The writer's directive toward his own text continuously orients and reorients *Walden* toward the pastoral mode, and, in Lindenberger's terms, contains the tensions that the book exhibits. For all the crosscurrents that ripple Walden's surface, Thoreau's pastoral imagination preserves "the equilibrium of the whole lake."

NOTES

1. See Walter Benn Michaels, "*Walden*'s False Bottoms," *Glyph: Johns Hopkins Textual Studies,* 1 (1977), 132–49.
2. R. W. B. Lewis, *The American Adam: Innocence, Tragedy, and Tradition in the Nineteenth Century* (Chicago: University of Chicago Press, 1955), p. 20.
3. H. Daniel Peck, *Thoreau's Morning Work: Memory and Perception in A Week on the Concord and Merrimack Rivers, the Journal, and Walden* (New Haven: Yale University Press, 1990), chap. 6.
4. Ibid.

5. See Friedrich von Schiller, *Naive and Sentimental Poetry and On the Sublime: Two Essays.* Trans. J. A. Elias (1800; reprinted New York: F. Ungar, 1966); William Empson, *Some Versions of Pastoral* (1935; reprinted New York: New Directions, 1950), p. 22. According to David M. Halperin, "the modern era [of considerations of pastoral] may be separated into two epochs, conveniently divided by the year 1800. That year saw the publication of Friedrich Schiller's final version of his essays on naive and sentimental poets . . . essays which laid the foundation for all recent thinking about pastoral" (*Before Pastoral: Theocritus and the Ancient Tradition of Bucolic Poetry* [New Haven: Yale University Press, 1983], p. 37).
6. Herbert Lindenberger, "The Idyllic Moment: On Pastoral and Romanticism," *College English,* 34(December 1972), 345.
7. Ibid., 338.
8. Ibid., 338, 340, 339.
9. James Fenimore Cooper, *The Deerslayer,* ed. James Franklin Beard (Albany: State University of New York Press, 1987), p. 149. For the pastoral dimension of *The Deerslayer* and of Cooper's other works, see my *A World by Itself: The Pastoral Moment in Cooper's Fiction* (New Haven: Yale University Press, 1977). For a ranging comparison of the pastoralism of Cooper and Thoreau, see John Seelye, "Some Green Thoughts on a Green Theme," *TriQuarterly,* 23/24(Winter-Spring 1972), 576–638.
10. D. H. Lawrence, *The Symbolic Meaning: The Uncollected Versions of Studies in Classic American Literature,* ed. Armin Arnold (New York: Viking, 1961), p. 106; Edmund Wilson, *The Shock of Recognition: The Development of Literature in the United States Recorded by the Men Who Made It,* 2d edition (New York: Grosset and Dunlap, 1955), p. 581.
11. See Leo Marx's highly influential study of American pastoralism, *The Machine in the Garden: Technology and the Pastoral Ideal in America* (New York: Oxford University Press, 1964), pp. 242–65 and passim. For Marx's reconsideration of some of the issues raised in this book, see his "Pastoralism in America," in *Ideology and Classic American Literature,* ed. Sacvan Bercovitch and Myra Jehlen (New York: Cambridge University Press, 1986), pp. 36–69. For challenges to Marx's formulations about American pastoralism in *The Machine in the Garden,* see Carolyn Porter, *Seeing and Being: The Plight of the Participant Observer in Emerson, James, Adams, and Faulkner* (Middletown, Conn.: Wesleyan University Press, 1981), pp. 69–82, 312–13; and Lawrence Buell, "American Pastoral Ideology Reappraised," *American Literary History,* 1(Spring 1989), 1–29.

12. For a vivid sense of just how commercially expansive and cosmopolitan Concord had become in Thoreau's time, see Robert A. Gross, "Transcendentalism and Urbanism: Concord, Boston, and the Wider World," *Journal of American Studies,* 18(1984), 361–81. See also Gross, "The Great Bean Field Hoax: Thoreau and the Agricultural Reformers," *Virginia Quarterly Review,* 6(Summer 1985), 483–97. For Thoreau's critique of modern farming, as this relates to "georgic" values in *Walden,* see James S. Tillman, "The Transcendental Georgic in *Walden,*" *ESQ,* 21(3d Quarter, 1975), 137–41.
13. Marx, *The Machine in the Garden,* pp. 220–1. In contrast, Nicolai Cikovsky, Jr., deemphasizes Inness's artistic transformations of the scene, arguing that "Lackawanna Valley" has "documentary accuracy." He also claims that Inness "does not condemn, but rather condones, even glorifies, the situation he represents" ("George Inness and the Hudson River School: The Lackawanna Valley," *American Art Journal,* 2[Fall 1970], p. 52). As the following analysis will make clear, my own view is closer to that of Marx. Barbara Novak attempts to reconcile Marx's and Cikovsky's views of "Lackawanna Valley." See her *Nature and Culture: American Landscape Painting, 1825–1875* (New York: Oxford University Press, 1980), pp. 171–4.
14. Marx, *The Machine in the Garden,* p. 221.
15. In this picture, the clouds reflect the hills in something of the way that Thoreau's beloved watery reflections, so often noted in his *Journal,* "answer" some of his own most valued landscapes. For an example, see Bradford Torrey and Francis H. Allen, eds., *The Journal of Henry David Thoreau* (Boston: Houghton Mifflin, 1906), vol. 3, p. 51.
16. For an important recent study of the complex ambivalences in Thoreau's works, including *Walden,* see Frederick Garber, *Thoreau's Fable of Inscribing* (Princeton: Princeton University Press, 1991).
17. For a compelling account of how, in *A Week,* Thoreau treats the lost civilization of Native Americans, see Robert F. Sayre, *Thoreau and the American Indians* (Princeton: Princeton University Press, 1977), chap. 2.
18. Renato Poggioli, *The Oaten Flute: Essays on Pastoral Poetry and the Pastoral Ideal* (Cambridge, Mass.: Harvard University Press, 1975), chap. 8.
19. Peck, *Thoreau's Morning Work,* chap. 5.
20. Martin Heidegger, "Building Dwelling Thinking," in *Poetry, Language, Thought,* trans. Albert Hofstadter (New York: Harper & Row, 1971), p. 145.
21. D. H. Lawrence, *Studies in Classic American Literature* (1923; reprinted New York: Viking Press, 1961), pp. 49, 60.

22. For example, see Robert Sattelmeyer, "Historical Introduction," *Journal 2: 1842–1848* (Princeton: Princeton University Press, 1984), p. 457.
23. *Journal* (1906 edition), vol. 3, pp. 214–15. For an illuminating psychoanalytic reading of this passage, see Richard Lebeaux, *Thoreau's Seasons* (Amherst: University of Massachusetts Press, 1984), pp. 45–6.
24. J. Lyndon Shanley, *The Making of Walden, with the Text of the First Version* (Chicago: University of Chicago Press, 1957).
25. For further discussion of *Walden*'s various "stories" of the self, see Peck, *Thoreau's Morning Work,* chap. 6. See also Robert Sattelmeyer, who writes of the way *Walden* dramatizes "the larger development of the narrator over the course of a decade of spiritual growth," creating the effect "of an earlier self subsumed but still present, as it were, within the later" ("The Remaking of *Walden,*" in *Writing the American Classics,* ed. James Barbour and Tom Quirk [Chapel Hill: University of North Carolina Press, 1990], p. 61).
26. Sherman Paul, *The Shores of America: Thoreau's Inward Exploration* (Urbana: University of Illinois Press, 1958), chap. 7.

5

Walden and the Politics of Contemporary Literary Theory

MICHAEL R. FISCHER

RICHARD Rorty seems to me right when he describes the central problem of contemporary theory as "the problem of how to overcome authority without claiming authority."[1] As I understand this problem, it results from the laudable desire of many contemporary theorists to challenge injustice and cruelty. Injustice can take many interconnected forms, from outright ethnocentrism, racism, and sexism to excluding certain works from the canon and certain people from the teaching profession. These forms of injustice typically pose as something higher – as, for example, the disinterested application of timeless aesthetic criteria or the rigorous insistence on objective standards. Contemporary literary theorists demystify these pious claims by exposing the ideological basis of all seemingly rational or neutral choices. From this point of view, all aesthetic preferences conceal political aims. They are not disinterested or pure but interested in keeping texts in their place, whether inside or outside the canon.

This insistence on the inescapability of ideology is meant to keep injustice from disguising itself as justice, but a problem arises when we want to argue that we have a better way of doing things – better than the arrangements we are criticizing. "Better" remains vague because the attack on purity seems to leave us with no positive terms for recommending our own position. Pressed to defend our alternatives, we slip into the rhetoric we have discredited, appealing to the very notions we have deconstructed (like truth, our common humanity, and reason). Our problem, as Rorty astutely puts it and as we have noted, is thus how to overcome authority without claiming it – without, in other words, reappropriating the vocabulary we have discredited. To adapt an often-cited remark of Audre Lorde's, how can we build our own house without borrowing the master's tools?[2]

I want to explore here how *Walden* speaks to this problem. In response to Lorde's warning that "the master's tools will never dismantle the master's house," Henry Louis Gates has recently urged that "*only* the master's tools will ever dismantle the master's house."[3] In what follows I see Thoreau adumbrating a comparable strategy – borrowing his neighbor's axe, for example, but sharpening it and using it to build something of his own. Building is a major concern of *Walden,* which is full of talk about tools, materials, and construction methods. Thoreau explains what his dwelling stands for but he also describes in great detail his getting it to stand – cutting and hewing six-inch-square timbers, digging a six-by-seven-foot cellar, and so on. He emphasizes what contemporary theorists might call his situatedness – occupying, even constructing, a specific place at a specific time. From this vantage point, he contests what his contemporaries find inevitable, true, and reasonable. He shows that it is possible to live and think another way. Is his way of life also necessary? In challenging the seemingly authoritative ideas and practices that bind his contemporaries, what kind of authority is Thoreau claiming for his own position?

In *America the Scrivener: Deconstruction and the Subject of Literary History,* Gregory S. Jay suspects that Thoreau claims necessity, truth, and universality for his own point of view. Focusing on Thoreau's opposition to the Mexican War and slavery, Jay zeroes in on a representative sentence from "Civil Disobedience": "I think that we should be men first, and subjects afterward." "We" presumably takes in everyone and provides an objective basis for criticizing what the government expects of us as subjects. In disobeying the government, we are heeding the dictates of our humanity. "Humanity," however, puts it too charitably for Jay. He thinks that by "men," Thoreau means men as opposed to women. Seized by "gender anxiety," Thoreau figures the failure of virtue "as a failure of masculinity."[4] The obedient subject is not dehumanized but emasculated. Civil disobedience is thus mandated not by our human nature but by

> a historically specific ideal of masculinity, which supplies [Thoreau] with the "higher law" he requires to justify his civil disobedience. . . . His own discourse thus repeats the very structure of patriarchal fidelity he condemns in his neighbors. This style of disobedience conforms to a rhetorical and ideological tradition which the mass of men recurrently invest in, either by deifying their patriarchs or by engaging in an oedipal rivalry with them. . . . Thoreau's recourse to the transcendental male constrains the play of his text and gives his address a "phallogocentric" destination.[5]

What looks like resistance turns out to be complicity with a repressive status quo.

Jay's reading allows me to reformulate the problem I posed at the outset. Jay is out to overcome authority, not just the authority of patriarchy but the authority of an American classic. He challenges Thoreau by historicizing his putative universal claims. What appears as a universal virtue – acting like a person instead of a machine – ends up an exclusionary, contingent norm bound up with the nineteenth-century understanding of masculinity and femininity. It is not clear, however, how Jay can improve on Thoreau, how he can reroute Thoreau's critique so it arrives at something other than a phallogocentric or otherwise undesirable destination. Undermining Thoreau's ground does not give Jay a better place to stand, which is perhaps why, when Jay aligns his criticism with "transgressive" work in literary and cultural studies, he immediately adds, "by 'transgressive' I do not mean 'subversive,' a word whose political connotations carry values I shall not claim."[6] "Transgressive" implies violating boundaries but not changing (that is, subverting) them. Jay's caution may stem from his inability to move from Thoreau's values to firmer ground.

I think Thoreau is committed to the subversiveness Jay shies away from. He wants to wake up his readers, not simply add zest to their daydreams.[7] His conviction that "we are sound asleep nearly half our time" is underwritten by his confidence that he knows what it means to be really awake, much as he purports to know truth from falsehood, necessity from accident, simplicity from unwarranted complexity, purity from contamination, fact from fiction, nature from artifice, freedom from slavery, and reality from appearance – to cite only some of the hierarchical distinctions he insists on. In a typical appeal to truth, Thoreau notes,

> I fear chiefly lest my expression may not be *extravagant* enough, may not wander far enough beyond the narrow limits of my daily experience, so as to be adequate to the truth of which I have been convinced. . . . I desire to speak somewhere *without* bounds; like a man in a waking moment, to men in their waking moments; for I am convinced that I cannot exaggerate enough even to lay the foundation of a true expression. (p. 324)

In this passage, as in many others, Thoreau claims to know the "soundest truths" and to anchor his argument in "what is inevitable and has a right to be" (p. 95).

Deconstructing truth claims such as these has almost become a reflex in contemporary theorists, like letting go of something hot. Whenever someone boasts of speaking "without bounds," we rush to uncover the social boundaries he unwittingly respects, as Jay does when he shows Thoreau's compliance with nineteenth-century masculinist prejudices. I would like to resist this temptation for a moment. Though Thoreau's apparent pontificating invites such a critique, he is not finally preaching to his readers from on high. In the passage I have cited, speaking without bounds is a desire, not an achievement, and needs to be reconciled with his conspicuous attempts to place himself in a self-constructed dwelling at a particular time beside Walden Pond. As mentioned earlier, Thoreau flaunts his situatedness, thereby anticipating critics who would hold it against his universal claims. He historicizes and personalizes his project: "We commonly do not remember that it is, after all, always the first person that is speaking. I should not talk so much about myself if there were anybody else whom I knew as well. Unfortunately, I am confined to this theme by the narrowness of my experience" (p. 3). He highlights his limitations: "I never knew, and never shall know, a worse man than myself" (p. 78), implicating himself in the quiet desperation he sees in his contemporaries.

Nevertheless, for all his awareness that he is presenting his own point of view, he still speaks with a universal voice, offering his opinions as if they were true for everyone.[8] He is willing to generalize on the basis of his own experience despite his admitted limitations: "If I seem to boast more than is becoming, my excuse is that I brag for humanity rather than myself; and my shortcomings and inconsistencies do not affect the truth of my statement" (p. 49). More strongly – and more disconcertingly – he suggests that because his opinions are his own (and not derived from outside himself, say from public opinion), they apply to others, too. "What is true for one is truer still for a thousand" (p.71), provided it is really true for one. Thoreau's ideas are somehow strengthened rather than limited by the fact that they originate in his personal experience. He speaks for others because he speaks for himself, not despite it.

Some early essays by Stanley Cavell help clarify what Thoreau is claiming here.[9] Cavell has long argued that Emerson and Thoreau underwrite ordinary-language philosophy, as practiced by J. L. Austin, Ludwig Wittgenstein, and Cavell himself. In different ways, these philosophers regard ordinary-language philosophy as a response to skepticism. By "skepticism," they mean the doubts that overtake us when we suspect we cannot know the external world or another person's mind. Ordinary-language philosophers are interested not in refuting skepticism (say by proving that the world exists) but in showing that skepticism arises when we use words in extraordinary ways. The cautious skeptic may want to say, for example, "I can only believe that someone is in pain; I cannot know it for sure." Ordinarily, faced with someone writhing in evident pain, we simply say, "He's in pain," if we say anything at all before helping him. In everyday life, "I can only believe he's in pain" would sound strange, even chilling. The ordinary-language philosopher explores our everyday confidence, as expressed in our ordinary speech, that we do know the world and the people in it. What entitles us to this confidence and what makes it always vulnerable to skeptical challenges are the major concerns of Austin, Wittgenstein, and Cavell.

In determining what we ordinarily say and, by extension, what sounds odd or queer, these philosophers do not empirically survey how people talk. In fact, Cavell explains, "one is not finally interested *at all* in how 'other' people talk, but in determining where and why one wishes, or hesitates, to use a particular expression oneself" (MWM, p. 99). The problem of course arises, "How can I speak for others on the basis of knowledge about myself?" (MWM, p. 67), or "Why are some claims about myself expressed in the form '*We* . . . '? About what can I speak for others on the basis of what I have learned about myself?" (MWM, p. 67).

Cavell does not so much answer these questions as deepen them. Citing a passage from Wittgenstein, Cavell concedes that human beings can be enigmas to one another. In a strange country, for example, we may find that we do not understand the people. Because we cannot speak to them, it follows that we cannot speak for them, leading Cavell to remark, "If speaking *for* someone else seems to be a mysterious process, that may be because speaking *to* someone does not seem mysterious enough" (MWM, pp. 67–8). "Mysterious enough" is a puzzling phrase (when is enough mystery enough?) and Cavell does not pause to elaborate on it, but he implies that we exaggerate the difficulty of speaking for others because we minimize or avoid all that is involved in speaking to them.

One of Thoreau's strangest passages in *Walden* also emphasizes the complexity of our speaking and listening to others. Thoreau regrets that the small size of his house forces him to be too close to his visitors. Close quarters are fine for "merely loquacious and loud talkers," who "can afford to stand very near together, cheek by jowl, and feel each other's breath" (p. 141). People who have something to say, however, people who are really speaking and listening to each other, need more space. Distance permits

> [their] thoughts to get into sailing trim and run a course or two before they make their port. The bullet of your thought must have overcome its lateral and ricochet motion and fallen into its last and steady course before it reaches the ear of the hearer, else it may plow out again through the side of his head. Also, our sentences wanted room to unfold and form their columns in the interval. Individuals, like nations, must have suitable broad and natural boundaries, even a considerable neutral ground, between them. (pp. 140–1)

Good fences apparently make good conversationalists. I do not see Thoreau warding off intimacy but enabling it by ensuring separateness. We can only come together if we are apart – if we exist as individuals. The loud, backslapping chattering that Thoreau describes does not constitute intimacy but counterfeits it. One prerequisite of intimacy involves revealing ourselves, or allowing ourselves to be seen. We can be too close to what we wish to see as well as too far away. It is as if the face-to-face talkers get physically close to one another in order to avoid being seen, much as they talk too loudly to avoid being heard. In any case, Thoreau's desire to speak without bounds – to speak for everyone – again must be placed against his wish to speak from within boundaries – to speak for himself. Thoreau accordingly says he preferred talking across the pond to his neighbors; when confined to his house, he and his visitors found themselves shoving their chairs farther and farther apart as their talk grew "loftier and grander." Even then "commonly there was not room enough" (p. 141).

Thoreau is constantly repositioning his readers in *Walden*, turning them around and unsettling their sense of space and time. On the one hand, faraway things turn out to be near: Slavery exists not just in the remote South but next door in Concord; miraculous changes occur every instant; heaven is under our feet; next to us the grandest laws are carried out everyday; the oldest Hindu and Egyptian philosopher merges into Thoreau; and the sacred water of the Ganges mingles with the pure water of Walden. On the other hand, nearness conceals distance: A nearby marching band seems "as far away as Palestine" (p. 161); familiar Concord can look as alien as a village of prairie dogs; inside oneself lie unknown continents and seas; and, in the passage mentioned above, standing cheek by jowl keeps two people miles apart, or at least fails to bring them together.

Miles contract and expand, years disappear, and moments last forever under mental pressure. By "mental pressure" I mean the pressure of a mind – Thoreau's mind – exploring itself. To a mind investigating itself, the distant past can feel fresh and the daily news already stale. In *Walden*, everything can be conducive to self-exploration but nothing has to be. If we follow our genius closely enough, "it will not fail to show [us] a fresh prospect every hour" (p. 112), but if we shy away from being our own Columbus (p. 321) nothing will automatically or necessarily compel us to explore ourselves. In getting to know ourselves, we can presumably profit from anything – housework, hoeing, sitting, poverty – but in our quiet desperation we can be impervious to everything: the wilderness, the best books, a splendid morning.

In comments like these, Thoreau may seem to underestimate the pull of circumstance or the power of our surroundings to sustain or thwart the introspection he values. He can fault us for allowing "only outlying and transient circumstances to make our occasions" (p. 134) instead of creating opportunities for ourselves. From his vantage point, "any prospect of awakening or coming to life to a dead man makes indifferent all times and places" (p. 134). Thoreau expresses this indifference when he professes to sit out the desperate games his contemporaries are playing. Exercising his mental freedom, he chooses "not to live in this restless, nervous, bustling, trivial Nineteenth Century, but stand or sit thoughtfully while it goes by" (pp. 329–30).

Nevertheless, even as he declares indifference to time and place, he acts as if circumstances matter, as when he complains that his cabin is too cramped for serious conversation. He presumably recommends a life of simplicity, industry, and economy, a life in the woods like his own, because it occasions self-discovery. Or perhaps, as I wondered at the outset, "recommends" is too strong a word. Maybe, in a carefree, take-it-or-leave-it spirit, he is only holding out his way of life as an option and asking his readers to count it as another possibility.

At stake here is not simply Thoreau's choice to live in the woods but his many opinions (freely offered on just about everything from the best time of day to eating meat and bearing firearms), not to mention his expectations for *Walden* itself. Thoreau clearly values self-exploration and self-emancipation. He wants his readers to think for themselves, to know their own minds. "Explore thyself" (p. 322), he tells us; "every path but your own is the path of fate. Keep on your own track, then" (p. 118). For Thoreau, everything follows from knowing and speaking your own mind – social justice as well as personal happiness – but what leads to this goal? How can *Walden?*

A similar problem arises in Cavell's commentary on Wittgenstein's *Philosophical Investigations*. Much as I have emphasized Thoreau's insistence that we know ourselves, Cavell finds exhortation in Wittgenstein – exhortation "not to belief, but to self-scrutiny"

(MWM, p. 71). Thoreau's "explore thyself" becomes Wittgenstein's "*look* and *see.*" As a response to such advice – if "advice" is not too weak a word – "belief is not enough" (MWM, 71). Wittgenstein wishes to prevent intellectual assent or understanding that "is unaccompanied by inner change" (MWM, p. 72). "In asking for more than belief," Cavell continues, a work like the *Investigations* "invites discipleship, which runs its own risks of dishonesty and hostility" (MWM, pp. 71–2).

> But I do not see that the faults of explicit discipleship are more dangerous than the faults which come from subjection to modes of thought and sensibility whose origins are unseen or unremembered and which therefore create a different blindness inaccessible in other ways to cure. Between control by the living and control by the dead there is nothing to choose. (MWM, p. 72)

Control by the living presumably lets us live, but achieving this control, or attracting disciples, remains a problem. For Wittgenstein, it is the problem of motivating others to go on with his work, or teaching them how to inherit it. As Cavell notes, there is no set of directions for doing ordinary-language philosophy: "Perhaps what is wanted really is a matter of conveying 'the hang' of something, and that is a very particular dimension of a subject to teach" (MWM, p. 103), an elusive dimension familiar to anyone trying to learn a new game or skill.

In a comparable spirit, when Thoreau addresses his writing to "poor students" (p. 4), he is not asking from them belief, or intellectual approval of his various opinions and his specific way of life. He insists that he "would not stand between any man and his genius" (p. 73) and I take him at his word.

> I would not have any one adopt *my* mode of living on any account; for, beside that before he has fairly learned it I may have found out another for myself, I desire that there may be as many different persons in the world as possible. (p. 71)

Thoreau notes "this is the only way, we say; but there are as many ways as there can be drawn radii from one centre" (p. 11). He leaves Walden, as if to discourage us from copying his experiment or taking it too literally. He similarly wants his writing to be endlessly suggestive and to defy our efforts to fix its meaning once and for all: "the volatile truth of our words should continually betray the inadequacy of the residual statement" (p. 325), the statement we can trap and take away in a paraphrase. Even his frequent appeals to nature are meant not to support his position but to bring out the limits of every viewpoint, his own included. "The universe is wider than our views of it" (p. 320): "It is a ridiculous demand which England and America make, that you shall speak so that they can understand you. . . . As if Nature could support but one order of understandings" (p. 324). Thoreau urges his readers to accept only "such portions [of *Walden*] as apply to them," trusting "that none will stretch the seams in putting on the coat, for it may do good service to him whom it fits" (p. 4). This one size needn't fit all, however. Other styles are not just possible but desirable.

In encouraging difference, Thoreau is asking for something other than belief in his many opinions. He does not simply allow for disagreement; he encourages it. He wishes us all to live "in view of the future or possible," that is to say "quite laxly and undefined in front, our outlines dim and misty on that side" (p. 324). Still, for all his flexibility and willingness to improvise, he is adamant about wanting his readers to do as he has done and explore themselves. He does not settle for something less than belief (tolerance, for instance) but seeks something more, something akin to the discipleship Cavell thinks Wittgenstein solicits. Self-knowledge is Thoreau's categorical imperative or, to borrow a metaphor from the chapter on economy, his bottom line. As I have already suggested, his problem is that, whereas nothing prevents self-scrutiny, nothing guarantees it either. He cannot force his readers to examine themselves and it is difficult to say what he can do above and beyond exhorting them.

Cavell's account of ordinary-language philosophy, as presented in "Austin at Criticism" and "The Availability of Wittgenstein's Later Philosophy" (two essays from *Must We Mean What We Say?*), sheds light on this problem. The ordinary-language philosopher – Cavell's chief examples are Austin and Wittgenstein – is in the awkward position of instructing others in what we ordinarily or naturally say. The position is awkward because we all presumably should know or at least decide for ourselves what we ordinarily say. Instead of offering arguments or describing how most people typically speak, ordinary-language philosophers ask their readers to do something – to *imagine*, for example, a language with two different words for negation;[10] to *ask* themselves what it means to believe in a theorem;[11] to *consider* the use of phrases analogous to "I know" and "I promise";[12] and to *suppose* that instead of saying "I know," I had said "I swear."[13] Extended examples – stories, really – prompt these invitations: "Imagine that you were telephoning someone and you said to him: 'This table is too tall,' and pointed to the table. What is the role of pointing here? Can I say: I *mean* the table in question by pointing to it?"[14]

In these stories, the philosopher is not just writing down conclusions but reaching them, arriving at what we ordinarily say instead of reporting on it. The reader is pictured not as a passive recipient of knowledge but as an essential partner in its production. In the example just mentioned, when Wittgenstein asks, "Can I say . . . ?" he is not asking for the reader's permission but for the reader's participation in his project. We can only answer the question by imagining examples of our own and thus engaging in the self-scrutiny he initiates. I might say that I can mean a table by pointing at it only when someone else can see my gesture, when, for instance, I point out to the movers the table I mean them to take to my new house. As Cavell puts it, Wittgenstein is "asking something which can be answered by remembering what is said and meant, or by trying out his own response to an imagined situation" (MWM, p. 64). Trying out Wittgenstein's response, like trying on *Walden* for size, emphasizes the exploratory, experimental response that Wittgenstein's writing invites.

Romantic writers – English as well as American – often call what they do experiments, as when Wordsworth, in the opening paragraph of his Preface to *Lyrical Ballads*, labels his poetry "an experiment, which, I hoped, might be of some use to ascertain how far, by fitting to metrical arrangement a selection of the real language of men in a state of vivid sensation, that sort of pleasure and that quantity of pleasure may be imparted, which a poet may rationally endeavor to impart."[15]

Thoreau, too, suggests that in *Walden* he is "trying the experiment of living" (p. 51) and, like a good empiricist, making discoveries "not by the synthetic but analytic process" (p. 62). Experiments succeed when others can duplicate them, and this is what Thoreau is trying to encourage in his readers – not necessarily to repeat what he has done but to do something similar. "For my part," he says, "I am glad to hear of experiments of this kind being tried; as that a young man tried for a fortnight to live on hard, raw corn on the ear, using his teeth for all mortar. The squirrel tribe tried the same and succeeded. The human race is interested in these experiments" (p. 65). Experiment, explore, try it out, see what happens – this is what he is urging his readers: "Man's capacities have never been measured; nor are we to judge of what he can do by any precedents, so little has been tried" (p. 10).

This is Thoreau's response to the problem I posed at the outset, the problem of overcoming authority without claiming the wrong kind of authority for oneself. By claiming "the wrong kind of authority," I mean laying down the law and avowing that some unimpeachable combination of human nature, God, and history is on our side. This is roughly what Jay accuses Thoreau of doing, but I see Thoreau inviting us to try on his universals for size, to see if they fit. He thus sets in motion the very critique Jay makes against him when he claims that Thoreau's idea of humanity is too narrow.

Much as the ordinary-language philosopher imagines examples, Thoreau sets one, hoping we will take him up on his invitation to consider what most of our trouble and anxiety is about, "and how much it is necessary that we be troubled, or, at least, careful" (p. 11). "Hoping" captures the vulnerability and value of his position. Invitations, after all, can be turned down, sometimes rudely. Accepting an invitation (as opposed, say, to obeying an order or agreeing with an argument) imposes a responsibility – in this case, the obligation to take part in the self-exploration Thoreau begins. To switch the metaphor, Thoreau notes that when he began his enterprise he borrowed an axe, but returned it sharper than he received it (p. 41).[16] He asks us, maybe challenges us, to do something similar: Borrow from *Walden* but use it to build something of our own.

There remains the problem of assessing the political value of Thoreau's writing. Again commenting on ordinary-language philosophy, Cavell notes "it is characteristic of work like Austin's – and this perhaps carries a certain justice – that criticism of it will often take the form of repudiating it as philosophy altogether" (MWM, p. 111). According to Cavell, this is exactly what has happened to Thoreau (and Emerson): Their writing has been rejected – Cavell sometimes says repressed – as philosophy by the very culture Cavell thinks they helped to found. One way to gauge the political potential of their writing is to think about the cost of the repression. To focus here only on Thoreau, what are we missing out on when we fail to receive his work as philosophy?

A quick answer to this question might be, "Nothing much," given what even a philosopher like Richard Rorty sees as the deservedly low cultural prestige of philosophy.[17] By "philosophy," however, Cavell does not mean an academic subject matter defined by where it is taught in a university or shelved in a library. He understands philosophy

> as a willingness to think not about something other than what ordinary human beings think about, but rather to learn to think undistractedly about things that ordinary human beings cannot help thinking about, or anyway cannot help having occur to them, sometimes in fantasy, sometimes as a flash across a landscape; such things, for example, as whether we can know the world as it is in itself, or whether others really know the nature of one's own experiences, or whether good and bad are relative, or whether we might not now be dreaming that we are awake, or whether modern tyrannies and weapons and spaces and speeds and art are continuous with the past of the human race or discontinuous, and hence whether the learning of the human race is not irrelevant to the problems it has brought before itself. Such thoughts are instances of that characteristic human willingness to allow questions for itself which it cannot answer. . . . [P]hilosophers after my heart will . . . wish to convey the thought that while there may be no satisfying answers to such questions *in certain forms*, there are, so to speak, directions to answers, *ways to think*, that are worth the time of your life to discover.[18]

Thoreau is clearly a philosopher after Cavell's heart. The passage just cited could be read as a gloss on Thoreau as I have been characterizing him. I think especially of Thoreau wondering whether we might be dreaming that we are awake, speculating whether we can look through each other's eyes (p. 10), skeptically asking "why do precisely these objects which we behold make a world?" (p. 225), and transvaluing terms like "good," "practical," "profitable," and "cost." The question then arises, What do we gain politically by reading him in this philosophical way?

The problem is how to judge in political terms writing that purports to transcend the cherished concerns of conventional politics: national boundaries (where I live, Thoreau says, "is as much Asia or Africa as New England" [p. 130]); revolutions (Thoreau apparently takes comfort from the fact that "the partridge and the rabbit are still sure to thrive, like true natives of the soil, whatever revolutions occur" [p. 281]); reform (self-styled reformers are for Thoreau "the greatest bores of all" [p. 154]); voting (famously criticized in "Civil Disobedience"); and institutions ("dirty institutions," Thoreau calls them, always out to "pursue and paw" a person and, "if they can, constrain him to belong to their desperate odd-fellow society" [p. 171]). It is easier to imagine Thoreau running from office than for it.

Even as Thoreau stakes out his independence from politics, however – "a simple and independent mind does not toil at the bidding of any prince. Genius is not a retainer to any emperor" (p. 57) – he claims that his writing makes a political difference. Writers apparently exercise the influence on society that political leaders vainly seek. The authors of the best books "are a natural and irresistible aristocracy in every society, and, more than kings or emperors, exert an influence on mankind" (p. 103). Instead of weakening his authority, Thoreau's distance from society somehow reinforces his impact on it, much as the space he puts between himself and his interlocutors enhances his communication with them. He escapes to the woods and writes not because he is indifferent to his contemporaries but because he cares about them. In his eyes at least, writing satisfies his obligations to others better than philanthropy and other, seemingly more direct, ways of achieving change.

A recent comment by Cavell on Wittgenstein helps clarify what Thoreau is claiming. As Cavell acknowledges, ordinary-language philosophy has often been accused of political conservatism. This accusation responds to various features of ordinary-language philosophy I cannot go into here, among them the apparent desire of the ordinary-language philosopher to reaffirm common sense and to ensure conformity to what "we" ordinarily say and do. Cavell suggests that Wittgenstein is working at a different level, asking us to accept, for example, not

> private property, but separateness; not a particular fact of power but the fact that I am a man, therefore of *this* (range or scale of) capacity for work, for pleasure, for endurance, for appeal, for command, for understanding, for wish, for will, for teaching, for suffering. The precise range or scale is not knowable a priori, any more than the precise range or scale of a word is to be known a priori. Of course you can *fix* the range; so can you confine a man or a woman, and not all the ways of senses of confinement are knowable a priori.[19]

Like Wittgenstein, Thoreau is urging us to investigate our capacities for each of the qualities mentioned here. Thoreau accordingly counters our complacent assumption that we already know our capacity for work ("labor of the hands," Thoreau discovers while hoeing, "has a constant and imperishable moral, and to the scholar it yields a classic result" [p. 157]); for trust ("I think we may safely trust a good deal more than we do" [p. 11]); for teaching ("shall the world be confined to one Paris or one Oxford forever?" [p. 109]); for self-limitation (the inhabitants of Concord seem to Thoreau "to be doing penance in a thousand remarkable ways" [p. 4]); and for the other qualities Cavell lists.

In suggesting that we cannot know once and for all our capabilities, Wittgenstein implies that we stand in need of what Cavell calls "something like transfiguration – some radical change, but as it were from inside, not *by* anything; some say in another birth, symbolizing a different order of natural reactions."[20] Cavell's vagueness – "something like transfiguration," "some radical change" – registers the difficulty of affixing a political label to writing that questions the sufficiency of politics.

I see nothing wrong with calling this writing philosophical (so long as we allow for the possibility that it might also be literary – and political), but classifying it does not solve the problem of assessing it. For me, this writing becomes dangerous when it trusts too much to the power of example and self-scrutiny, as when Thoreau says

> I believe that what so saddens the reformer is not his sympathy with his fellows in distress, but, though he be the holiest son of God, is his private ail. Let this be righted, let the spring come to him, the morning rise over his couch, and he will forsake his generous companions without apology. (p. 78)

Leaving aside for the moment Thoreau's reductionist and unfair psychologizing, I hear him implying that if the reformer reforms himself, he will not only forsake reform but will somehow be of more help to his fellows in distress. "Somehow" is dangerously vague and opens the door to complacency, as does Thoreau's assurance that some of our fellows in distress are only apparently suffering ("Often the poor man is not so cold and hungry as he is dirty and ragged and gross. It is partly his taste, and not merely his misfortune" [p. 75]). Thoreau's self-concern sometimes degenerates into self-absorption, or inattention to the circumstances of his contemporaries and his own material advantages. When he boasts that no children crying disturbed the silence of his cabin, the parent in me wishes they had. Maybe then he would have understood why John Field "heaved a sigh" (p. 206) at Thoreau's advice that he and his family live simply and go a-huckleberrying in the summer for their amusement.

At his best, however, Thoreau is not so much cynical about reform as reluctant to overrate it. He argues that it needs to be supplemented, not scrapped – complemented by the self-reform he favors. Go ahead and give money to the poor, but "spend yourself with it, and do not merely abandon it to them" (p. 75). Oppose Southern slavery, but attend to your own emancipation. Thoreau is thus constantly challenging us to go further, to bring our political convictions home, and not let changing the world excuse us from changing ourselves. Nothing relieves us from the mandate to examine ourselves, not even the right kind of politics: "No method nor discipline can supersede the necessity of being forever on the alert. What is a course of history of philosophy, or poetry, no matter how well selected, or the best society, or the most admirable routine of life, compared with the discipline of looking always at what is to be seen?" (p. 111)

We need to read Thoreau for the same reason he says "we need the tonic of wildness" (p. 317): "We need to witness our own limits transgressed, and some life pasturing freely where we never wander" (p. 318). So much of contemporary criticism is devoted to cutting down spurious universals to size, showing what they exclude, silence, or otherwise repress. In Thoreau's case, we tame his apparent wildness and show him to be grounded in a particular time and place as well as a specific ideology instead of pasturing freely. This is a valuable activity that Thoreau himself engages in when he unmasks the provincialism and narrowness of his contemporaries.[21] But pointing out the limitations of someone else's position does not guarantee we will be sensitive to the limitations of our own. According to Thoreau, nothing guarantees self-awareness or exempts us from the necessity of being forever on the alert. By encouraging ceaseless self-scrutiny, Thoreau challenges oppositional thinking to go far enough.

NOTES

1. Richard Rorty, *Contingency, Irony, and Solidarity* (Cambridge: Cambridge University Press, 1989), p. 105.
2. Audre Lorde writes, "The master's tools will never dismantle the master's house." For a typical citation of her statement, see Ellen Rooney, *Seductive Reasoning* (Ithaca: Cornell University Press, 1989), pp. 11, 251.
3. Henry Louis Gates, Jr., "Critical Remarks," *Anatomy of Racism*, ed. David Theo Goldberg (Minneapolis: University of Minnesota Press, 1990), p. 326.
4. Gregory S. Jay, *America the Scrivener* (Ithaca: Cornell University Press, 1990), p. 18.
5. Ibid., p. 19
6. Ibid., p. xi.
7. I paraphrase here an early letter from Matthew Arnold to Arthur Hugh Clough: "I am glad you like the Gipsy Scholar – but what does it *do* for you? . . . 'The complaining millions of men / Darken in labour and pain' – what they want is something to *animate* and *ennoble* them – not merely zest to their melancholy or grace to their dreams. – I believe a feeling of this kind is the basis of my nature –

and of my poetics." It is also the basis of Thoreau's hopes for *Walden.* H. L. Lowry, ed., *The Letters of Matthew Arnold to Arthur Hugh Clough* (New York: Oxford University Press, 1932), p. 146.

8. "With a universal voice" is Immanuel Kant's phrase from his *Critique of Judgment,* where he argues that in making aesthetic judgments, we act as if we can make a rightful claim upon everyone's assent even though our judgment is not (strictly speaking) cognitive. Kant goes to great lengths to show why this "subjective universality" is not a contradiction in terms. I think Thoreau goes further than Kant in claiming truth for his aesthetic and ethical judgments. Even so, "subjective universality" captures the provisional kinds of universals Thoreau advocates. Stanley Cavell notes a parallel between Kant's "universal voice" and the ordinary-language philosopher's claims about what we ordinarily say – claims that I argue help to illuminate Thoreau's *Walden.* See Stanley Cavell, *Must We Mean What We Say?* (1969; reprinted Cambridge: Cambridge University Press, 1976), p. 94. Subsequent references are cited as MWM and inserted in the text.
9. Cavell is best known in Thoreau circles for his *The Senses of Walden* (1972; reprinted San Francisco: North Point Press, 1981), which I discuss at length in my *Stanley Cavell and Literary Skepticism* (Chicago: University of Chicago Press, 1989), Chapter 5. I discuss here Cavell's work on ordinary-language philosophy, claiming that many of the things he says about Ludwig Wittgenstein and J. L. Austin also fit Thoreau.
10. Ludwig Wittgenstein, *Philosophical Investigations,* trans. G. E. M. Anscombe (New York: Macmillan, 1953), #556.
11. Ibid., #578.
12. J. L. Austin, *Philosophical Papers,* 3d ed. (Oxford: Oxford University Press, 1979), p. 101.
13. Ibid., p. 101.
14. Wittgenstein, *Philosophical Investigations,* #670.
15. William Wordsworth, "Preface to the Second Edition of *Lyrical Ballads,*" *Critical Theory Since Plato,* ed. Hazard Adams (New York: Harcourt Brace Jovanovich, 1971), p. 433.
16. Thoreau's stated reason for borrowing the axe – "It is difficult to begin without borrowing, but perhaps it is the most generous course thus to permit your fellow-men to have an interest in your enterprise" (pp. 40–1) – sounds disingenuous to me, meant to protect his vaunted self-sufficiency. Thoreau typically shies away from examining his dependency on others – from the acquaintances who assist him in setting up the frame of his house (p. 45) to the "priceless domestic"

(p. 141) who helps keep it clean. His practice, if not his doctrine, suggests to me that it is impossible to begin without borrowing but that indebtedness need not preclude innovation.

17. For further discussion of Rorty's devaluation of philosophy – and apparent promotion of literature – see my "Redefining Philosophy as Literature: Richard Rorty's 'Defence' of Literary Culture," in *Reading Rorty*, ed. Alan Malachowski (Oxford: Basil Blackwell, 1990), pp. 233–43.
18. Stanley Cavell, *Themes Out of School* (San Francisco: North Point Press, 1984), p. 9.
19. Stanley Cavell, *This New Yet Unapproachable America* (Albuquerque: Living Batch Press, 1989), p. 44.
20. Ibid., p. 44.
21. Cavell calls such unmasking perhaps "*the* modern intellectual art" and goes on to say, "if, as one supposes, this modern art develops with the weakening or growing irrelevance of given conventions and institutions, then the position of the unmasker is by its nature socially unhinged, and his responsibility for his position becomes progressively rooted in his single existence" (MWM, 112). I see this happening already in Thoreau.

Notes on Contributors

Lawrence Buell is a Professor of English and American Literature and Language at Harvard University. He is the author of *Literary Transcendentalism: Style and Vision in the American Renaissance* (1973) and *New England Literary Culture, from Revolution through Renaissance* (1986).

Michael R. Fischer is a Professor of English at the University of New Mexico, Albuquerque. He is the author of *Does Deconstruction Make Any Difference: Poststructuralism and the Defense of Poetry in Modern Criticism* (1985) and *Stanley Cavell and Literary Skepticism* (1989).

Anne LaBastille, of the Adirondack Park, New York, is a free-lance writer and consulting ecologist. She is the author of *Woodswoman* (1976) and its sequel *Beyond Black Bear Lake* (1987), *Women and Wilderness* (1980), *Mama Poc* (1990), and *The Wilderness World of Anne LaBastille* (1992).

H. Daniel Peck is Professor of English and Director of the American Culture Program at Vassar College. He is the author of *A World by Itself: The Pastoral Moment in Cooper's Fiction* (1977) and *Thoreau's Morning Work* (1990). He is also editor of the Cambridge University Press *New Essays on The Last of the Mohicans.*

Robert F. Sayre is a Professor of English at the University of Iowa. He is the author of *The Examined Self* (1964 & 1988) and *Thoreau and the American Indians* (1977).

Selected Bibliography

The now generally accepted standard text of *Walden*, which is also used for all quotations in this volume, is the one edited by J. Lyndon Shanley for the Modern Language Association–Center for Editions of American Authors edition of *The Writings of Henry D. Thoreau* (Princeton: Princeton University Press, 1971). The text usually earlier taken as definitive was the one in the twenty-volume "Walden edition" of Thoreau's Writings (Boston: Houghton Mifflin, 1906). Another accurate text is in the Library of America Thoreau volume (*A Week, Walden, The Maine Woods, Cape Cod*), edited by Robert F. Sayre (1985). This volume also includes notes identifying quotations and allusions. *The Variorum Walden*, edited by Walter Harding (Twayne Publishers, 1962; Washington Square Press, 1963), contains over seventy-five pages of informative annotations, and *The Annotated Walden*, edited by Philip Van Doren Stern (New York: C. N. Potter, Inc., 1970) is also useful. For concordances, see J. Stephen Sherwin and Richard C. Reynolds, *A Word Index to Walden with Textual Notes* (Charlottesville: University of Virginia Press, 1960), and Marlene Ogden, *Walden, A Concordance* (New York: Garland, 1985).

Discussion of biographies of Thoreau can be found in the general introduction to this collection of essays. For additional biographical information readers should turn first to his *Journal*, using the new Princeton edition where possible and otherwise the 1906 Houghton Mifflin edition, and to *The Correspondence of Henry David Thoreau*, edited by Walter Harding and Carl Bode (New York: New York University Press, 1958). *A Thoreau Gazetteer*, ed. Robert F. Stowell and William L. Howarth (Princeton: Princeton University Press, 1970) prints maps and photographs of Concord, Walden Pond, and other places where Thoreau traveled.

For a comprehensive review of research and criticism on Thoreau and *Walden*, Walter Harding and Michael Meyer's *The New Thoreau Handbook* (New York: New York University Press, 1980) is indispensable. Also useful is Lewis Leary's chapter on Thoreau in *Eight American Authors*, edited by James Woodress (New York: Norton, 1971). For annual updates of research, see *American Literary Scholarship* (Durham, N.C., 1963–) and the *Thoreau Society Bulletin* (Geneseo, New York, 1941–).

There are a number of informative and convenient collections of essays on Thoreau and *Walden:*

Thoreau: A Century of Criticism, ed. Walter Harding. Dallas: Southern Methodist University Press, 1954.

Approaches to Walden, ed. Lauriat Lane, Jr. San Francisco: Wadsworth Publishing Co., 1961.

Thoreau: A Collection of Critical Essays, ed. Sherman Paul. Englewood Cliffs, N.J.: Prentice-Hall, 1962.

Thoreau in Our Season, ed. John Hicks. Amherst: University of Massachusetts Press, 1966.

Walden and Civil Disobedience: Authoritative Texts, Background, Reviews, and Essays in Criticism, ed. Owen Thomas. Norton Critical Editions. New York: W. W. Norton & Co., 1966.

Twentieth Century Interpretations of Walden, ed. Richard Ruland. Englewood Cliffs, N.J.: Prentice-Hall, 1968.

The Recognition of Henry David Thoreau, ed. Wendell Glick. Ann Arbor: University of Michigan Press, 1969.

The Merrill Studies in Walden, ed. Joseph Moldenhauer. Columbus, Ohio: Charles E. Merrill Publishing Co., 1971.

Thoreau: A Symposium, ed. Joseph McElrath, Jr. *ESQ: A Journal of the American Renaissance* 19(1973), 131–99.

Henry David Thoreau, ed. Harold Bloom. New York: Chelsea House, 1987.

Critical Essays on Henry David Thoreau's Walden, ed. Joel Myerson. Boston: G. K. Hall & Co., 1988.

In this chronological list the volumes edited by Harding, Glick, Thomas, and Myerson begin with reprints of nineteenth-century reviews and articles. The others contain only twentieth-century material.

For further perspectives, including ones not mentioned in the Introduction to this volume, the serious reader of *Walden* should also consult the following modern critical studies.

Anderson, Charles. *The Magic Circle of Walden.* New York: Columbia University Press, 1968.

Buell, Lawrence. *Literary Transcendentalism: Style and Vision in the American Renaissance.* Ithaca: Cornell University Press, 1973.

Burbick, Joan. *Thoreau's Alternative History: Changing Perspectives on Nature, Culture, and Language.* Philadelphia: University of Pennsylvania Press, 1987.

Cameron, Sharon. *Writing Nature.* Cambridge: Harvard University Press, 1987.

Cavell, Stanley. *The Senses of Walden: An Expanded Edition.* San Francisco: North Point Press, 1981.

Fischer, Michael R. *Stanley Cavell and Literary Skepticism.* Chicago, University of Chicago Press, 1989.

Garber, Frederick. *Thoreau's Redemptive Imagination.* New York: New York University Press, 1977.

Gozzi, Raymond D., ed. *Thoreau's Psychology: Eight Essays.* Lanham, Md.: University Press of America, 1983.

Hildebidle, John. *Thoreau: A Naturalist's Liberty.* Cambridge: Harvard University Press, 1983.

McIntosh, James. *Thoreau as Romantic Naturalist: His Shifting Stance Toward Nature.* Ithaca: Cornell University Press, 1974.

Neufeldt, Leonard N. *The Economist: Henry Thoreau and Enterprise.* New York: Oxford University Press, 1989.

Peck, H. Daniel. *Thoreau's Morning Work: Memory and Perception in A Week on the Concord and Merrimack Rivers, the Journal, and Walden.* New Haven and London: Yale University Press, 1990.

Porte, Joel. *Emerson and Thoreau: Transcendentalists in Conflict.* Middletown, Conn.: Wesleyan University Press, 1966.

Richardson, Robert D., Jr. *Henry Thoreau: A Life of the Mind.* Berkeley and Los Angeles: University of California Press, 1986.

Sattelmeyer, Robert. *Thoreau's Reading: A Study in Intellectual History.* Princeton: Princeton University Press, 1988.

Sayre, Robert F. *Thoreau and the American Indians.* Princeton: Princeton University Press, 1977.

Schneider, Richard J. *Henry David Thoreau.* Twayne's United States Authors Series. Boston: G. K. Hall & Co., Twayne Publishers, 1987.

"Thoreau and Nineteenth-Century American Landscape Painting." *ESQ: A Journal of the American Renaissance* 3(1985): 67–88.

West, Michael. "Scatology and Eschatology." *PMLA* 89(1974): 1043–64.